Conditional Futurism

Conditional Futurism

New Perspective of End-Time Prophecy

JAMES GOETZ

RESOURCE *Publications* • Eugene, Oregon

CONDITIONAL FUTURISM
New Perspective of End-Time Prophecy

Copyright © 2012 James Goetz. All rights reserved. Except for brief quotations in critical publications or reviews, no part of this book may be reproduced in any manner without prior written permission from the publisher. Write: Permissions, Wipf and Stock Publishers, 199 W. 8th Ave., Suite 3, Eugene, OR 97401.

Resource Publications
An Imprint of Wipf and Stock Publishers
199 W. 8th Ave., Suite 3
Eugene, OR 97401
www.wipfandstock.com

ISBN 13: 978-1-60899-866-1
Manufactured in the U.S.A.

Scriptures taken from the Holy Bible, New International Version®, NIV®. Copyright © 1973, 1978, 1984, 2011 by Biblica, Inc.™ Used by permission of Zondervan. All rights reserved worldwide. www.zondervan.com.

The "NIV" and "New International Version" are trademarks registered in the United States Patent and Trademark Office by Biblica, Inc.™

To Laurie, Julie Anne, Christiana, Jeremy, and Joshua.

If at any time I announce that a nation or kingdom is to be uprooted, torn down and destroyed, and if that nation I warned repents of its evil, then I will relent and not inflict on it the disaster I had planned.

—The Lord in Jeremiah 18:7–8, New International Version

If I say to a wicked person, 'You will surely die,' but they then turn away from their sin and do what is just and right—if they give back what they took in pledge for a loan, return what they have stolen, follow the decrees that give life, and do no evil—that person will surely live; they will not die.

—The Lord in Ezekiel 33:14–15

Therefore, Your Majesty, be pleased to accept my advice: Renounce your sins by doing what is right, and your wickedness by being kind to the oppressed. It may be that then your prosperity will continue.

—Daniel speaking to King Nebuchadnezzar in Daniel 4:27

"Men's courses will foreshadow certain ends, to which, if persevered in, they must lead," said Scrooge. "But if the courses be departed from, the ends will change. Say it is thus with what you show me."

—Charles Dickens

Contents

Acknowledgments ix

1 Conditional Futurism in Sum 1

2 Interpretation of End-Time Prophecy 6

3 Genesis and the Mosaic Covenant 10

4 The Davidic Dynasty and Psalms 18

5 Isaiah 28

6 Jeremiah 42

7 Prince Gog from the Land of Magog 48

8 Zechariah 55

9 Daniel 61

10 The Gospels 83

11 Acts 117

12 Letters of Paul and Hebrews 123

13 Letters of Peter, John, and Jude 132

14 The Eighth King in Revelation 143

15 Judgment, the Kings of the Earth, and the Nations in Revelation 156

Bibliography 167
Subject Index 171
Author Index 173
Ancient Document Index 174

Acknowledgments

I WROTE THIS BOOK for both a general audience and a scholarly audience. I used the reader-friendly New International Version for biblical quotations on behalf of the general audience while I strove for the accuracy of all biblical interpretation regardless of the Bible translation. I also avoided the use of most abbreviations and explained basic biblical concepts for the sake of the general audience. Moreover, my original contribution to theological scholarship involves the development of the end-time theology (eschatology) called *conditional futurism*.

I thank the staff at Wipf and Stock, my volunteer proofreaders, my volunteer reviewers/endorsers, Dale Brueggemann for important criticism of previous writings related to this book, Robin Parry for encouraging me in my writing and making an important suggestion for the direction of this book, Keith Wells for extensive copy editing of chapters 1–11, and Laurie Goetz for persevering two decades of my efforts at writing.

1

Conditional Futurism in Sum

APOCALYPSE MEANS "REVELATION" OR "uncovering." Biblical apocalypses such as the book of Revelation describe divine visions or dreams filled with symbolism about important future events that involve miraculous intervention while a divinely appointed mediator helps to interpret the vision.[1] Many Christian scholars hold to traditional futurism, which teaches that the apocalypse in Revelation prophesied unconditional judgments about the end times.[2] For example, Revelation 19 prophesied that the beast and the false prophet would oppose the Lord and be thrown into the lake of fire forever. Traditional futurists teach that this prophetic judgment against the beast and false prophet is unconditional; that is, nothing could alter the general outcome of the beast and false prophet opposing the Lord and being thrown into the lake of fire forever. However, careful study of biblical prophecy indicates that the *outcome* of any prophetic judgment is conditional; this is, the disobedient audience of the prophecy could genuinely repent and alter the outcome of the judgment.[3] The word and purposes of the Lord never alter while the outcome of the word of the Lord can vary.

Biblical passages that teach about conditions in prophetic judgments include the apocalypse in Daniel 4 and classical prophecies

---

1. Scholars debate the definition of *apocalyptic literature* while most definitions include the elements of a divine vision or dream filled with symbolism about important future events that involve miraculous intervention and a divinely appointed mediator who helps to interpret the vision.

2. The term *end times* refers to events leading to the end of human history, which climaxes with the return of the Lord. And the academic term *eschatology* involves the study of end-time prophecy.

3. See Kearley, "The Conditional Nature of Prophecy."

such as Jeremiah 18:1–10 and Ezekiel 33:13–16. Daniel 4:19–27 describes Daniel interpreting an apocalypse dreamt by Babylonian king Nebuchadnezzar:

> [19] Then Daniel (also called Belteshazzar) was greatly perplexed for a time, and his thoughts terrified him. So the king said, "Belteshazzar, do not let the dream or its meaning alarm you."
>
> Belteshazzar answered, "My lord, if only the dream applied to your enemies and its meaning to your adversaries! [20] The tree you saw, which grew large and strong, with its top touching the sky, visible to the whole earth, [21] with beautiful leaves and abundant fruit, providing food for all, giving shelter to the wild animals, and having nesting places in its branches for the birds— [22] Your Majesty, you are that tree! You have become great and strong; your greatness has grown until it reaches the sky, and your dominion extends to distant parts of the earth.
>
> [23] "Your Majesty saw a holy one, a messenger, coming down from heaven and saying, 'Cut down the tree and destroy it, but leave the stump, bound with iron and bronze, in the grass of the field, while its roots remain in the ground. Let him be drenched with the dew of heaven; let him live with the wild animals, until seven times pass by for him.'
>
> [24] "This is the interpretation, Your Majesty, and this is the decree the Most High has issued against my lord the king: [25] You will be driven away from people and will live with the wild animals; you will eat grass like the ox and be drenched with the dew of heaven. Seven times will pass by for you until you acknowledge that the Most High is sovereign over all kingdoms on earth and gives them to anyone he wishes. [26] The command to leave the stump of the tree with its roots means that your kingdom will be restored to you when you acknowledge that Heaven rules. [27] Therefore, Your Majesty, be pleased to accept my advice: Renounce your sins by doing what is right, and your wickedness by being kind to the oppressed. It may be that then your prosperity will continue."
> (Daniel 4:19–27)

In these verses, Daniel interpreted the symbols in the apocalypse dreamt by Nebuchadnezzar. The Most High, who is God, decreed that Nebuchadnezzar would live like a wild animal for seven periods of time until he would acknowledge that God is sovereign over the kingdoms of the earth.⁴ This implied that Nebuchadnezzar would lose his throne for seven periods of time. Daniel in verse 4:27 also interpreted that Nebuchadnezzar could repent and alter the outcome of the decree of God in this apocalyptic judgment. Also, this apocalyptic dream included no explicit conditions for the judgment while Daniel interpreted implicit conditions in the judgment.⁵

The scenario in Daniel 4 agrees with Jeremiah 18:1–10 and Ezekiel 33:13–16 teaching that genuine repentance of a wicked nation or a wicked person alters the outcome of a prophetic judgment. For instance, Jeremiah 18:1–10 describes the Lord, who is God, teaching Jeremiah about the conditional nature of both prophetic blessings and prophetic judgments:

> ¹ This is the word that came to Jeremiah from the LORD: ² "Go down to the potter's house, and there I will give you my message." ³ So I went down to the potter's house, and I saw him working at the wheel. ⁴ But the pot he was shaping from the clay was marred in his hands; so the potter formed it into another pot, shaping it as seemed best to him.
>
> ⁵ Then the word of the LORD came to me. ⁶ He said, "Can I not do with you, Israel, as this potter does?" declares the LORD. "Like clay in the hand of the potter, so are you in my hand, Israel. ⁷ If at any time I announce that a nation or kingdom is to be uprooted, torn down and destroyed, ⁸ and if that nation I warned repents of its evil, then I will relent and not inflict on it the disaster I had planned. ⁹ And if at another time I announce that a nation or kingdom is to be built up and planted, ¹⁰ and if it does evil in my sight and does not obey me, then I will reconsider the good I had intended to do for it. (Jeremiah 18:1–10)

In these verses, the Lord directed Jeremiah to observe the work of a potter. Jeremiah saw the potter make a clay pot with defects in the structure. Then, the potter used the same clay to start over and make another pot, which presumably lacked defects. Next, the Lord compared himself to the potter while the Lord compared the Israelite kingdom of Judah to the clay used to make pots. After that, the Lord in Jeremiah

---

4. The seven periods of time could mean "seven years" or "seven indefinite periods of time."

5. I introduced this interpretation of Daniel 4:19–27 in "The Conditional Apocalypse of King Nebuchadnezzar," *TheoPerspectives* (blog), February 11, 2009, http://theoperspectives.blogspot.com/2009/02/conditional-apocalypse-king.html.

18:7–10 expanded the illustration to include any possible nation at any given time. The Lord declared that any time that he announces a judgment of destruction against any nation, then that nation could repent and avoid the destruction. For instance, the Lord in Jeremiah 27:1–11 announced judgments against the nations of Edom, Moab, Ammon, Tyre and Sidon. Also, verses 18:1–10 teach that at any time that the Lord announces a special blessing in favor of any nation, then that nation could turn to evil and lose the special blessing. This teaching in 18:1–10 implies conditions in all prophetic blessings and prophetic judgments to the nations. Likewise, prophetic blessings and prophetic judgments to nations need no explicit statement of conditions while they always include implicit conditions. In all cases, the word of the Lord proves true regardless of the outcome.

Ezekiel 33:13–16 parallels Jeremiah 10:1–10 by teaching about the conditions of prophetic blessings and prophetic judgments to individual people:

> [13] If I tell a righteous person that they will surely live, but then they trust in their righteousness and do evil, none of the righteous things that person has done will be remembered; they will die for the evil they have done. [14] And if I say to a wicked person, 'You will surely die,' but they then turn away from their sin and do what is just and right— [15] if they give back what they took in pledge for a loan, return what they have stolen, follow the decrees that give life, and do no evil—that person will surely live; they will not die. [16] None of the sins that person has committed will be remembered against them. They have done what is just and right; they will surely live. (Ezekiel 33:13–16)

Ezekiel 33:13–16 teaches that the Lord could prophesy that a righteous person would surely live, but the righteous person would lose the special blessing of life if he turns to evil. Also, the Lord could prophesy to a wicked person, "You will surely die," but the wicked person could turn away from evil and live. These verses also imply that particular prophetic blessings and prophetic judgments need no statement of explicit conditions while they always include implicit conditions.

The Bible includes many other cases of conditional prophecy. For example, the book of Jonah taught that God pronounced a judgment of destruction against the city of Nineveh. The prophetic word of judgment against Nineveh included no explicit conditions while repentance of the people of Nineveh altered the outcome of the prophetic word.

This book introduces a paradigm-shifting interpretation of the end times called *conditional futurism*. Conditional futurism proposes conditional judgments in end-time prophecy including conditions in the apocalyptic judgment of the final antichrist, also called *the man of lawlessness* and *an eighth king*.[6] Likewise, the proposal of conditional end-time judgments challenges the unconditional judgments of traditional futurism. And the proposal of a final antichrist challenges other end-time theologies such as preterism and idealism. For instance, full preterism says that events from AD 30 to 70 completely fulfilled all prophecies in Revelation while idealism says that the prophecies in Revelation apply to all periods of time with no focus on the return of the Lord.

Conditional futurism also works with the belief that Jesus Christ inaugurated the kingdom of God on earth during his first-century ministry while Christ will consummate the kingdom when he returns. For example, Christ associated the kingdom with his preaching of God's word while he also taught about fulfilling the kingdom when he returns.[7]

The next chapter outlines principles of biblical interpretation (hermeneutics). Then, the book interprets selections of the Christian Bible from Genesis to Revelation that focus on topics related to the end times including (1) conditions in divine covenants and prophecy, (2) messianic prophecy, (3) the kingdom of God, and (4) end-time judgments.[8] I show biblical evidence supporting that conditional futurism is the best interpretation of end-time prophecy. I also show that most of the evidence agrees with traditional futurism, while critical points distinguish between traditional futurism and conditional futurism.

---

6. See "the man of lawlessness" in 2 Thessalonians 2:1–12 and "an eighth king" in Revelation 17:8–11.

7. See chapter 10 and Ladd, *The Presence of the Future*.

8. The Christian Bible divides into the Old Testament written by Jews (Israelites) before the earthly life of Jesus Christ and the New Testament written during the lifetime of the first followers of Christ. Messianic prophecy is Old Testament prophecy about the Messiah (Christ) and the messianic age.

2

Interpretation of End-Time Prophecy

CONDITIONAL FUTURISM INCLUDES MANY mainstream principles for interpreting end-time prophecy and the rest of the Bible. For instance, conditional futurism assumes the original manuscripts of the Bible are the authoritative written word of God. The Spirit of God inspired the writing of the Bible while all of the teachings are true within the original ancient Mediterranean context.[1]

Conditional futurism also assumes that some biblical prophecies have multiple fulfillments. For example, Revelation 17:9–11 teaches about multiple fulfillments of the beast who has "seven heads":

> [9] This calls for a mind with wisdom. The seven heads are seven hills on which the woman sits. [10] They are also seven kings. Five have fallen, one is, the other has not yet come; but when he does come, he must remain for only a little while. [11] The beast who once was, and now is not, is an eighth king. He belongs to the seven and is going to his destruction. (Revelation 17:9–11)

A mind with wisdom can understand that *the seven heads* represents both "seven hills" and "seven kings." The *seven hills* in Revelation 17:9 refers to the Seven Hills of Rome while the *seven kings* in 17:10 refers to Roman emperors. Also, 17:11 teaches that the beast also represents "an eighth king." Likewise, these verses teach that the prophecy of the seven heads includes at least three fulfillments: (1) Rome, (2) a series of Roman emperors, and (3) a final eighth Roman emperor.

This reference to Rome and Roman emperors also illustrates the biblical concepts of *prefiguration* and *postfiguration*. A prefiguration foreshadows a future person, place, or event while a postfiguration analogizes a previous person, place, or event. In this case, Revelation

---

1. See Ramm, *Protestant Biblical Interpretation*.

14–18 on six occasions figuratively refers to "Babylon" as the capital city of governmental persecution that opposes Christians. This Babylon was the capital city of the Neo-Babylonian Empire, which in 597 BC sacked Jerusalem and in 586 BC destroyed Jerusalem.[2] However, Revelation 17:9–10 identifies "Rome" as the capital city that opposes Christians. Likewise, Revelation conflated symbolic references of both Babylon and Rome to describe governmental persecution that opposes Christians. Babylon was a prefiguration of Rome while Rome was a postfiguration of Babylon. Some scholars alternatively use the terms *type* for prefiguration and *antitype* for postfiguration, while the study of biblical prefiguration and postfiguration (type and antitype) is called *typology*.

Important principles for interpreting end-time prophecy include understanding the concepts of prefiguration, postfiguration, and prophecy with multiple fulfillments. Also, these concepts help both traditional futurism and conditional futurism incorporate many valid ideas from alternate end-time theologies such as preterism and idealism.[3]

Interpretation of end-time prophecy also requires an appreciation for figures of speech and symbolism. For instance, many of the symbols in Revelation refer to the teachings of Jesus and the Old Testament. Also, the Gospel writers record Jesus using figures of speech such as hyperbole in Mark 9:43–48:

> [43] If your hand causes you to stumble, cut it off. It is better for you to enter life maimed than with two hands to go into hell, where the fire never goes out. [45] And if your foot causes you to stumble, cut it off. It is better for you to enter life crippled than to have two feet and be thrown into hell. [47] And if your eye causes you to stumble, pluck it out. It is better for you to enter the kingdom of God with one eye than to have two eyes and be thrown into hell, [48] where "the worms that eat them do not die, and the fire is not quenched." (Mark 9:43–48[4])

---

2. Jerusalem was the capital city of ancient Israel/Judah and is the capital city of modern day Israel.

3. As noted earlier, full preterism says that events in AD 70 completely fulfilled all prophecies in Revelation while idealism says that the prophecies in Revelation apply to all periods of time.

4. The New International Version of the Bible excludes Mark 9:44 and 9:46 because these verses are the same as verse 9:48 and are nonexistent in the earliest known manuscripts of Mark.

Mark 9:43–48 records Jesus telling people that in some cases of sin they might need to cut off their hand or foot or pluck out their eye. No Christian teacher including the most conservative literalist ever suggested that these verses taught that in some cases of sin Christians need to literally cut off their hand or foot or pluck out their eye. These verses encourage Christians to take drastic measures to avoid sinning while those drastic measures never include actual self-mutilation. This is a clear case of Jesus using hyperbole. Likewise, the Bible like all other literature requires careful analysis of figures of speech.

Another important principle for interpreting end-time prophecy includes understanding the biblical precedence that prophecy can be written for both the original audience and future generations. For example, 1 Peter 1:10–12 teaches that prophets in the Old Testament wrote messianic prophecy for future generations:

> [10] Concerning this salvation, the prophets, who spoke of the grace that was to come to you, searched intently and with the greatest care, [11] trying to find out the time and circumstances to which the Spirit of Christ in them was pointing when he predicted the sufferings of the Messiah and the glories that would follow. [12] It was revealed to them that they were not serving themselves but you, when they spoke of the things that have now been told you by those who have preached the gospel to you by the Holy Spirit sent from heaven. Even angels long to look into these things. (1 Peter 1:10–12)

Daniel included apocalyptic messianic prophecy, and 1 Peter 1:10–12 implied that the audience of Danielic prophecy went beyond the original audience to include future generations. Likewise, interpretation of biblical apocalypses should consider the original audience while also considering later audiences.

Sound interpretation of end-time prophecy also includes understanding biblical precedence that prophetic judgments include conditions. For instance, as explained in chapter 1, Daniel 4 taught about the implicit conditions in the respective apocalypse dreamt by King Nebuchadnezzar.

In sum, conditional futurism interprets end-time prophecy with the following principles:

1. The Bible is the written word of God and must be understood in its original context.
2. Prophecy sometimes has multiple fulfillments and might include prefiguration and postfiguration.
3. The audience of prophecy includes the original audience and future audiences.
4. Some of the language in the Bible includes symbolism and figures of speech that could include hyperbole.
5. Prophetic judgments such as end-time judgments include conditions.

3

Genesis and the Mosaic Covenant

THE GARDEN OF EDEN

MANY CASES OF END-TIME prophecy in the New Testament refer back to the Old Testament. For example, Revelation 22 refers to the Garden of Eden in Genesis 2:4–3:24 while prophesying about the restoration of the Edenic tree of life in heaven.

Highlights of the Genesis 2:4–3:24 narrative include the following:

1. The Lord God created the heavens and the earth.

2. The Lord formed the body of a man named Adam and breathed life into him.

3. The Lord planted a garden in Eden with beautiful trees bearing delicious and nutritious fruit.

4. In the middle of the garden, the Lord made the tree of life and the tree of the personal knowledge of good and evil.[1]

5. A theophany of the Lord educated Adam by telling him that he may eat from any tree in the garden except for the tree of the personal knowledge of good and evil because eating from that tree causes death.[2]

6. The Lord made Adam a wife named *Eve* while the couple enjoyed nakedness together without shame.

---

1. The phrase the tree of the knowledge of good and evil from Genesis 2:9 and 2:17 referred to more than abstract knowledge of good and evil. For instance, the respective Hebrew word for knowledge implied personal knowledge.

2. A theophany in Christianity is a tangible appearance of God while theophanies sometimes include human-like bodily characteristics.

7. The serpent, craftier than any other wild animal, approached Eve and tricked her into believing that she would never die if she ate the forbidden fruit from the tree of the personal knowledge of good and evil.
8. Eve ate the forbidden fruit and gave some to Adam who also ate it.
9. Adam and Eve felt shame about their nakedness and sowed leaves together into clothing.
10. Adam and Eve heard the familiar sound of the theophany walking in the garden while they hid themselves.
11. The Lord confronted Adam about the forbidden fruit.
12. Adam blamed his God-given wife for giving him the fruit.
13. Eve blamed the serpent for tricking her into eating the fruit.
14. The Lord spoke a punishing curse to the serpent, which included a prophecy that a descendent of Eve would crush the head of the serpent.
15. The Lord spoke a punishing curse to both Eve and Adam.
16. The Lord comforted Adam and Eve by making animal skin garments for them.
17. The Lord banished Adam and Eve from the Garden of Eden and the tree of life.

Regardless of controversies about the authorship and the literalness or nonliteralness of Genesis 2:4—3:24,[3] points of end-time prophecy in this narrative include (1) human access to the tree of life, (2) humans relating with a theophany, (3) the importance of divinely established conditions for blessings and curses, and (4) the offspring of Eve crushing the head of the serpent.

The restriction against eating from the tree of the personal knowledge of good and evil represented a condition for blessings and curses. Obeying the restriction would result in the blessing of endless access to divine paradise while disobeying would eventually result in the curse of death.

---

3. See LaSor et al., *Old Testament Survey*, chapter 2.

Genesis 3:14–15 summarizes the titanic battle between the serpent and the offspring of Eve:

> ¹⁴ So the LORD God said to the serpent, "Because you have done this,
> "Cursed are you above all livestock
> and all wild animals!
> You will crawl on your belly
> and you will eat dust
> all the days of your life.
> ¹⁵ And I will put enmity
> between you and the woman,
> and between your offspring and hers;
> he will crush your head,
> and you will strike his heel."
> (Genesis 3:14–15)

These verses describe the theophany in the Garden of Eden pronouncing a curse on the serpent because of the serpent's disobedience and destruction of the first humans. Revelation 12:9 teaches that this ancient serpent is the devil. And the theophany in the garden foreshadowed both the earthly life of Jesus and the appearance of God to man in heaven.

The phrase *crawl on your belly* in Genesis 3:14 symbolically implied limited mobility while the reference to eating dust referred to death.[4] The enmity between the woman's offspring and the serpent's offspring in 3:15 represented the titanic battle between the devil's forces and humanity, especially Jesus. One meaning of the phrase *he will crush your head* implied that Christ would cause a fatal injury to the devil while the phrase *you will strike his heel* implied that the devil would cause a temporary injury to Christ. And the injury to Christ would include the temporary death of Christ while the fatal injury to the devil would include the devil's final defeat.

GENESIS 6–9

Genesis 6–9 teaches about the judgment of the great flood in the days of Noah. In the flood account, the wickedness of humanity increased and God pronounced judgment on all humanity except the righteous family of Noah. God planned to flood the earth and told Noah to build an ark

---

4. For instance, Genesis 3:19 described death as returning to dust.

to protect his family and two of each kind of land animal from the flood. Noah built the ark, and then, his family and all the chosen land animals entered the ark. God flooded the earth with rain for forty days while all humans and land animals on the earth died and everybody in the ark lived. Finally, the waters subsided; God blessed Noah and his family to prosper and multiply on the earth; God made a covenant with Noah and all living creatures that God would never again destroy all life with a flood.

Second Peter 2:5 describes Noah as a preacher of righteousness who God spared from the flood. This might indicate that Noah preached to his contemporaries about God's judgment and turning to righteous. Anybody could have turned from wickedness to righteousness and enjoyed protection from the flood. Likewise, regardless of the controversies in Genesis 6–9, the flood account teaches about the universal human tendency to sin and God's conditional judgment.

One of the controversies in the flood account involves Genesis 6:1–4 and the enigmatic "sons of God" who married any beautiful "daughters of humans" who pleased them, while the sons of God and daughters of humans propagated the "Nephilim." Traditional interpretation identifies these sons of God as angels who rebelled against God by marrying and impregnating human women. Additionally, the apocalyptic 1 Enoch elaborates on these verses and says that the Nephilim were a hybrid race of giants. I propose instead that these Nephilim were not biological hybrids but humans because their fathers were angelophanies with human bodies,[5] which I elaborate on in chapter 13.

GENESIS 12

Genesis 12:1–3 taught more about the offspring of Eve and related blessings and curses:

> [1] The LORD had said to Abram,
> "Go from your country, your people
> and your father's household to the land I will show you.
> [2] "I will make you into a great nation,
> and I will bless you;
> I will make your name great,

---

5. An angelophany is an appearance of an angel that is visible to one or more humans. Biblical examples of angelophanies with evidently human bodies include the appearance of angels in Genesis 18–19.

and you will be a blessing.
³ I will bless those who bless you,
and whoever curses you I will curse;
and all peoples on earth
will be blessed through you."
(Genesis 12:1–3)

These verses narrated the Lord calling Abram, who in Genesis 17:5 is famously renamed *Abraham*. Abram grew up in the second millennium BC as a Mesopotamian polytheist, but in Genesis 12:1–3 the Lord called Abram to leave his polytheistic family traditions and go to a new land while worshiping only the Lord.[6] The Lord promised to bless Abram and make him into a great nation. Abram would turn into a pivotal figure in human history while everybody who blesses him would be blessed and everybody who curses him would be cursed. Ultimately, all people in the earth would be blessed through Abram, while the primary blessing through him to all people turned out to be his most famous descendant, Jesus of Nazareth.

This call of Abram began the Abrahamic Covenant, an agreement between the Lord and Abram/Abraham. The Lord set a covenantal condition for Abram and made covenantal promises to him. The Lord required Abram to leave his country, polytheistic family traditions, and go to a new land while the Lord promised to bless Abram and make him a blessing to all people on earth.

After the call of Abram, he took his family and possessions to travel to Canaan, which includes the land of modern day Israel. Then, the Lord appeared to Abram and said that his offspring would inherit the land.[7]

GENESIS 15

The Abrahamic Covenant progressed in Genesis 15. For example, the Lord and Abram talked with each other while the Lord made a covenant with Abram. This covenant resembled an ancient Near Eastern royal

---

6. Polytheists believe in and worship multiple gods while monotheists believe in only one God. Abram presumably lived in Mesopotamia during the Old Babylonian period (the twentieth to fifteenth centuries BC) while precise or imprecise dates of events in his life have no impact on messianic prophecy and end-time prophecy. Also, the land of Mesopotamia was the cradle of civilization and is currently modern day Iraq.

7. See Genesis 12:4–7.

grant that involved a king granting land and unconditional protection to a loyal servant.

In Genesis 15:1–6, the Lord appeared to Abram in a vision and encouraged him to be fearless while the Lord promised to protect and reward him. Abram responded by confiding his fear to the Lord. Abram feared his old age and childlessness because he thought that a mere servant in his house would inherit his estate. Then, the Lord promised that Abram would have a child from his own body, and his descendants would be as numerous as the stars in the sky on a clear night. Abram believed the Lord while the Lord regarded Abram as righteous.

In Genesis 15:7–8, the Lord spoke again to Abram while repeating that the Lord called him to leave Mesopotamia and take possession of Canaan. Then, Abram questioned how he could know that he would take the land.

In Genesis 15:9–11, the Lord responded by requesting that Abram bring the Lord a three-year-old cow, a three-year-old female goat, a three-year-old ram, a dove, and a young pigeon. Abram brought these animals to the Lord, cut the mammals in two, and arranged the halves opposite each other. Birds of prey tried to attack the sacrificed animals. But Abram protected the sacrifices and drove away the birds.

In Genesis 15:12–16, during sunset, Abram fell into a deep sleep. Then, the Lord spoke to Abram about his descendants becoming enslaved and the eventual exodus from slavery with great possessions.

In Genesis 15:17–18, when the darkness of night set, a smoking firepot and blazing torch suddenly appeared and passed between the halves of the sacrificed mammals. That day, the Lord made a covenant with Abram and promised the land of Canaan to Abram's descendants.[8]

The sacrificial cutting of the mammals in half resembled a typical part of Ancient Near Eastern covenants. In this case, Abram did the work of supplying the animals and cutting the mammals while the Lord made the covenantal promise to Abram. And the apparent unconditional promise implied the loyalty of Abram.

GENESIS 17

The Lord in Genesis 17 made another covenant with Abram. The Lord appeared to Abram when he was ninety-nine years old. Then, the Lord

---

8. Genesis 15:17–18.

demanded faithfulness from Abram while the Lord promised a covenant with him. The Lord promised to make Abram a father of many nations and changed Abram's name to *Abraham*.[9] And the Lord promised to establish an everlasting covenant with Abraham and his descendants. The Lord promised to be their God and give them the land of Canaan.

The covenant involved the circumcision of all males in the household and descendancy of Abraham who are eight days and older.[10] And the Lord said that all uncircumcised males would be cut off from the covenantal promises.

The Lord in Genesis 17 also said that Abraham's ninety-year-old wife Sarai renamed *Sarah* would finally enjoy her first natural child.[11] Then, Abraham and all males in his household were circumcised to affirm the covenant. Within a year, Abraham and Sarah enjoyed the birth of their first and only child, Isaac. And all of the promises and conditions of the covenant passed down to Isaac.

The covenants in Genesis 12, 15, and 17 are typically referred to as the Abrahamic Covenant. Also, according to Genesis 25:19–34 and 27:1–40, the covenant excluded Isaac's son (Abraham's grandson) Esau while the covenant passed down to Isaac's son and Esau's twin brother Jacob. Additionally, the Lord in Genesis 32:22–32 famously renamed Jacob to *Israel*. And ten sons and two grandsons of Jacob/Israel developed into the twelve political tribes of the nation of Israel: Reuben, Simeon, Judah, Issachar, Zebulun, Ephraim, Manasseh, Benjamin, Dan, Asher, Gad, and Naphtali.[12]

THE MOSAIC COVENANT

Israel and his sons moved from Canaan to Egypt and lived there for several generations while multiplying into a large number of people called the *Israelites*. Eventually, an Egyptian Pharaoh enslaved the Israelites. However, the Lord raised up an Israelite named *Moses* to deliver the

---

9. Abram means "exalted father" while Abraham means "father of many."

10. Circumcision involves cutting off the fold of skin at the end of the male genital.

11. Both Sarai and Sarah mean "princess."

12. Numbers 1:1–16 listed the twelve political tribes of Israel. Jacob/Israel fathered twelve sons: Reuben, Simeon, Levi, Judah, Dan, Naphtali, Gad, Asher, Issachar, Zebulun, Joseph, and Benjamin (Genesis 29:32—35:18). Ten of these sons and two grandsons from his son Joseph became the patriarchs of the twelve political tribes. And Israel's son Levi became the patriarch of the Israelite priesthood called the Levitical priesthood.

Israelites from Egyptian slavery. And the Lord led the Israelites to Mount Sinai in the Sinai Peninsula to make a covenant with them.[13]

The Lord first told Moses the terms of the covenant, which is called the *Mosaic Covenant*. In this covenant, the Lord declared that he was the Lord God of the Israelites. He reestablished his promise made to the Israelite forefather Abraham that his descendants would inherit the land of Canaan. Also, the Lord required that the Israelites obey many commands beginning with the Ten Commandments. Likewise, the Lord made a conditional covenant with Moses and the Israelites.[14]

The Mosaic Covenant also established the Israelite high priesthood and the Levitical priesthood. For example, Moses and his brother Aaron belonged to the Israelite tribe of Levi while the Lord made the Levites the priestly tribe. The Lord also made Aaron the high priest while descendants of his would succeed him as high priest. The Lord asked Moses to anoint (smear with oil) Aaron and his sons for the priesthood; the anointing represented being chosen and empowered by the Lord.[15]

A major part of the high priest ministry originally involved altar sacrifices in front of the tabernacle (tent). And Solomon's temple eventually incorporated all biblical rituals related to the tabernacle. Both the tabernacle and the temple represented the presence of the Lord while many prophecies involved references to the temple.

The Lord also made a special covenant with Phinehas, the grandson of Aaron. The Lord in Numbers 25:12–13 said:

> [12] Therefore tell him I am making my covenant of peace with him. [13] He and his descendants will have a covenant of a lasting priesthood, because he was zealous for the honor of his God and made atonement for the Israelites. (Numbers 25:12–13)

Some say that the Phinehas covenant is an unconditional covenant for a lasting priesthood. However, Babylonian king Nebuchadnezzar temporarily terminated the ministry of the high priesthood and Zechariah prophesied that the restoration of the high priesthood depended upon the obedience of the high priest, which chapters 5, 6, and 8 discuss.

---

13. The Sinai Peninsula is the Asian region of Egypt. Its western borders are the Suez Canal and the Gulf of Suez. Its northern border is the Mediterranean Sea. And its eastern border includes Israel.

14. See Exodus, Leviticus, Numbers, and Deuteronomy.

15. See Exodus and Leviticus.

4

The Davidic Dynasty and Psalms

THE DAVIDIC DYNASTY

AROUND 1000 BC, THE Lord chose David from the tribe of Judah and made him the king of Israel. The Lord promised David that one of his descendants would rule from his throne forever. This promise called *the Davidic covenant* also foreshadowed the rule of the Messiah in the messianic age. This covenant included conditions requiring obedience while some Davidic rulers turned disobedient, which resulted in the end of the Davidic dynasty in 586 BC until the birth of Jesus.

The Lord first made Saul the first king of Israel in the mid-eleventh century BC. This transformed the confederation of Israel's twelve political tribes into the united monarchy of Israel. But Saul disobeyed prophetic direction from the Lord. Consequently, the Lord pronounced the eventual end of Saul's kingship and the eventual beginning of David's kingship.[1]

After the pronouncement of David's kingship, while Saul continued to reign, David performed mighty feats while his popularity among the Israelites soared. For instance, David slew a giant enemy soldier named Goliath. Saul turned envious against David and tried to kill David three times. And Saul finally died in a battle.[2]

Soon after the death of Saul, the tribe of Judah crowned David the king of Judah. The other eleven tribes of Israel made a son of Saul named *Ish-Bosheth* the king of Israel. During the next two years, the armies of David fought against the armies of Ish-Bosheth while David defeated Ish-Bosheth. After the defeat of Ish-Bosheth, the Lord made David the

---

1. See 1 Samuel 8:1—16:13.
2. See 1 Samuel 16:14—31:13.

king of Israel, restoring the united monarchy of Israel. Then, David conquered the city of Jerusalem near the northern border of the land of Judah, and David made Jerusalem the capital of Israel.[3]

After David built his palace in Jerusalem and secured peace from neighboring people, he planned to build a temple for the Lord in Jerusalem. But the Lord told David that he should not build the temple, although a son of David would succeed him as king and build the temple. The Lord also promised David that one of his descendants would rule from his throne forever.[4] For example, the Lord prophesied through Nathan to David:

> [8] "Now then, tell my servant David, 'This is what the LORD Almighty says: I took you from the pasture, from tending the flock, and appointed you ruler over my people Israel. [9] I have been with you wherever you have gone, and I have cut off all your enemies from before you. Now I will make your name great, like the names of the greatest men on earth. [10] And I will provide a place for my people Israel and will plant them so that they can have a home of their own and no longer be disturbed. Wicked people will not oppress them anymore, as they did at the beginning [11] and have done ever since the time I appointed leaders over my people Israel. I will also give you rest from all your enemies.
>
> "'The LORD declares to you that the LORD himself will establish a house for you: [12] When your days are over and you rest with your ancestors, I will raise up your offspring to succeed you, your own flesh and blood, and I will establish his kingdom. [13] He is the one who will build a house for my Name, and I will establish the throne of his kingdom forever. [14] I will be his father, and he will be my son. When he does wrong, I will punish him with a rod wielded by men, with floggings inflicted by human hands. [15] But my love will never be taken away from him, as I took it away from Saul, whom I removed from before you. [16] Your house and your kingdom will endure forever before me; your throne will be established forever.'" (2 Samuel 7:8–16)

In these verses, the Lord made David the king of Israel in place of Saul because of Saul's unfaithfulness and David's faithful heart for the Lord. And the Lord promised to establish David's throne forever.

This might appear as an unconditional promise. For instance, the Lord says that he would punish a wayward successor to the Davidic

---

3. See 2 Samuel 1:1—5:10.
4. See 2 Samuel 7:1–17.

throne, but the Lord would never take away his love from a Davidic successor as he did from Saul. However, biblical history proves that some aspects of the promise were figurative instead of literal.

David himself fell into disobedience and suffered punishments similar to the pronouncement in 2 Samuel 7:12-16. David committed adultery with Bathsheba and impregnated her. After David failed to cover up the pregnancy, David secretly murdered Bathsheba's husband. David also took a census of his soldiers in disobedience to the Lord. David repented of these sins and suffered greatly while keeping his throne.[5]

Shortly before David died, David gave the rule of his kingdom to his son Solomon. The compiler of 1 Chronicles and 2 Chronicles portrays the reigns of David and Solomon as the Golden Age of Israel. At first, Solomon reverenced the Lord, gained great wisdom, built a glorious temple for the Lord and a glorious palace for himself, and gained great political power.

However, Solomon married many foreign princesses in the quest for political power while the Lord forbade intermarriage with some of these princesses. The Lord forbade intermarriages with women from various nations while the Lord warned that women from those nations would tempt Israelite men into polytheistic worship, including temple prostitution and child sacrifice. Such polytheistic worship severely violated Israelite biblical law. Despite Solomon's renown in the Golden Age, when he grew old, he built polytheistic temples for his foreign wives who offered sacrifices to polytheistic deities. Solomon divided his heart between the Lord and the foreign deities of his wives.[6]

The Lord responded to Solomon's disobedience by pronouncing that Solomon's royal successor, his son Rehoboam, would lose ten of the twelve tribes of Israel from his kingdom, a temporary discipline for the Davidic dynasty. But Solomon showed no sign of repenting from polytheism.[7]

After Solomon died, the Israelites crowned his son Rehoboam the king of Israel. He blundered in diplomacy early in his reign, which instigated a rebellion from ten tribes of Israel. Those ten tribes made Jeroboam the king of Israel, according to a prophecy from the Lord.[8]

---

5. See 2 Samuel 11:1—1 Kings 2:12.
6. See 1 Kings 11:1-13.
7. See 1 Kings 11:9-43.
8. See 1 Kings 12:1-24.

This began the age of the divided monarchy: the kingdom of Judah ruled by the Davidic dynasty and the Northern Kingdom of Israel ruled by various northern Israelites.

A series of twenty kings reigned over the Northern Kingdom until Assyria captured the capital of the kingdom in 722 BC and dispersed the northern Israelites into exile. The Lord allowed Assyria to destroy the Northern Kingdom because the Israelites disobeyed the Lord—for example, worshiping golden calves and polytheistic deities, practicing divination and sorcery, and sacrificing their children at altars.[9]

A series of twenty Davidic kings beginning with Rehoboam ruled over the kingdom of Judah until 586 BC when Nebuchadnezzar of Babylon destroyed Jerusalem. A few notable kings of Judah obeyed the Lord—for example, Asa, Jehoshaphat, Uzziah, Jotham, Hezekiah, and Josiah. However, most of the kings of Judah disobeyed the Lord by worshiping polytheistic deities, including King Ahaz and King Manasseh who both sacrificed and burned sons in the Jerusalem Valley of Ben Hinnom. Likewise, chronic disobedience to the Lord caused the destruction of Jerusalem and the end of the Davidic dynasty for about 580 years until the birth of Jesus of Nazareth.[10]

PSALM 89

Psalm 89, evidently written during the Babylonian exile, reflected upon the Lord's promise to establish David's throne forever and grieved the end of the Davidic throne. Psalm 89:1–4 began with praise to the Lord and referred to the Davidic promise:

> ¹ I will sing of the LORD's great love forever;
> with my mouth I will make your faithfulness known
> through all generations.
> ² I will declare that your love stands firm forever,
> that you have established your faithfulness in heaven itself.
> ³ You said, "I have made a covenant with my chosen one,
> I have sworn to David my servant,
> ⁴ 'I will establish your line forever
> and make your throne firm through all generations.'"
> (Psalm 89:1–4)

After Psalm 89:1–4 praised the Lord and quoted from the Davidic promise, then 89:5–18 continued to praise the Lord while focusing on

---

9. See 1 Kings 12:25—2 Kings 17:23.
10. See 1 Kings 11:43—2 Kings 25:7 and 2 Chronicles 9:31—36:21.

the mighty strength of the Lord. Then, 89:19–37 referred back to the Davidic promise:

> [19] Once you spoke in a vision,
> to your faithful people you said:
> "I have bestowed strength on a warrior;
> I have raised up a young man from among the people.
> [20] I have found David my servant;
> with my sacred oil I have anointed him.
> [21] My hand will sustain him;
> surely my arm will strengthen him.
> [22] The enemy will not get the better of him;
> the wicked will not oppress him.
> [23] I will crush his foes before him
> and strike down his adversaries.
> [24] My faithful love will be with him,
> and through my name his horn will be exalted.
> [25] I will set his hand over the sea,
> his right hand over the rivers.
> [26] He will call out to me, 'You are my Father,
> my God, the Rock my Savior.'
> [27] And I will appoint him to be my firstborn,
> the most exalted of the kings of the earth.
> [28] I will maintain my love to him forever,
> and my covenant with him will never fail.
> [29] I will establish his line forever,
> his throne as long as the heavens endure.
> [30] "If his sons forsake my law
> and do not follow my statutes,
> [31] if they violate my decrees
> and fail to keep my commands,
> [32] I will punish their sin with the rod,
> their iniquity with flogging;
> [33] but I will not take my love from him,
> nor will I ever betray my faithfulness.
> [34] I will not violate my covenant
> or alter what my lips have uttered.
> [35] Once for all, I have sworn by my holiness—
> and I will not lie to David—
> [36] that his line will continue forever
> and his throne endure before me like the sun;
> [37] it will be established forever like the moon,
> the faithful witness in the sky."
> (Psalm 89:19–37)

Psalm 89:19–37 described the Lord's promise to David while foreshadowing the arrival of the Messiah. And as stated earlier, 89:5–18 praised the mighty strength of the Lord. Then, 89:19–29 proclaimed that the Lord used his might to strengthen King David. And 89:27 declared that the Lord made David the "firstborn" of the Lord, a prefiguration of the Lord sending the messianic Son of God. And 89:30–33 recounted the prophetic warning of temporary punishments for disobedient Davidic rulers while 89:34–37 affirmed that the Lord made an everlasting covenant with David and his descendants.

Psalm 89:38–52 grieved the end of the Davidic throne during the Babylonian exile while the psalmist hoped and prayed for the restoration of the Davidic dynasty:

> 38 But you have rejected, you have spurned,
> you have been very angry with your anointed one.
> 39 You have renounced the covenant with your servant
> and have defiled his crown in the dust.
> 40 You have broken through all his walls
> and reduced his strongholds to ruins.
> 41 All who pass by have plundered him;
> he has become the scorn of his neighbors.
> 42 You have exalted the right hand of his foes;
> you have made all his enemies rejoice.
> 43 You have turned back the edge of his sword
> and have not supported him in battle.
> 44 You have put an end to his splendor
> and cast his throne to the ground.
> 45 You have cut short the days of his youth;
> you have covered him with a mantle of shame.
> 46 How long, O LORD? Will you hide yourself forever?
> How long will your wrath burn like fire?
> 47 Remember how fleeting is my life.
> For what futility you have created all men!
> 48 What man can live and not see death,
> or save himself from the power of the grave?
> 49 O Lord, where is your former great love,
> which in your faithfulness you swore to David?
> 50 Remember, Lord, how your servant has been mocked,
> how I bear in my heart the taunts of all the nations,
> 51 the taunts with which your enemies have mocked, O LORD,
> with which they have mocked every step of your anointed one.
> 52 Praise be to the LORD forever!
> Amen and Amen.
> (Psalm 89:38–52)

Despite the everlasting promise made to David according to Psalm 89:1–37, the psalmist in verses 89:38–45 grieved the Lord's rejection of the last Davidic king. And as stated earlier, in 89:30–33, the Lord required a condition of obedience within the everlasting promise to David. And the chronic disobedience of most Davidic kings caused the cessation of the dynasty. However, the psalmist kept hope in the restoration of the Davidic dynasty. And a half millennium later, the Lord found favor with a righteous couple named Joseph and Mary in the lineage of David while Mary gave birth to Jesus. Also, the phrase *anointed one* in 89:38 and 89:51 related to the Hebrew word *Messiah* and the Greek word *Christ*.

THE NATIONS AND KINGS IN PSALMS

Important motifs in Psalms and end-time prophecy includes the words *nations* and *kings*. In Psalms, the word *nations* appears seventy-two times while the word *kings* appears twenty-six times. For instance, as noted earlier, Psalm 89:27 declares that the Lord appointed King David as the firstborn of the Lord and made him "the most exalted of the kings of the earth." This section reviews the use of *nations* and *kings* in selections from Psalms.

Psalm 2

Psalm 2 includes both the word *nations* and the phrase *kings of the earth*. Psalm 2:1–3 says:

> ¹ Why do the nations conspire
> and the peoples plot in vain?
> ² The kings of the earth rise up
> and the rulers band together
> against the LORD and against his anointed, saying,
> ³ "Let us break their chains
> and throw off their shackles."
> (Psalm 2:1–3)

The psalmist wrote Psalm 2 evidently for the coronation of a Davidic king referred to as "his anointed." The scene of the nations conspiring and the kings of the earth taking their stand referred to a typical scene in the Ancient Near East when subject kings challenged the rule of a newly coronated supreme king, testing the strength of the new king. As described earlier, an example of subjects challenging the rule of a new king occurred soon after the coronation of King Rehoboam when he lost the rule over ten tribes of Israel.

Also, Psalm 2:7–8 describes the Lord offering "the nations" as an inheritance to the Davidic king:

> ⁷ I will proclaim the LORD's decree:
> He said to me, "You are my son;
> today I have become your father.
> ⁸ Ask me,
> and I will make the nations your inheritance,
> the ends of the earth your possession.
> (Psalm 2:7–8)

The Lord declared the sonship of the Davidic king and offered him "the nations" of the earth as an inheritance. This offer of the nations went far beyond the offer of Canaan promised to Abram/Abraham according to Genesis 12:1–3 and Genesis 15, as stated earlier in chapter 3. And the Davidic line in Old Testament history never approached the supreme rule of the Ancient Near East, let alone the entire earth. Perhaps the magnitude of this offer and the scene in Psalm 2:1–2 represented both hyperbole for the Davidic coronation and the potential for the expansion of the Davidic kingdom. Also, the expansion required the conditions of (1) asking the Lord for the nations and (2) obedience to the Lord according to the Davidic promise. Moreover, only Jesus literally fulfills 2:7–8.

Psalm 2 described contrasting views of the nations. On one hand, as noted earlier in Psalm 2:1–2, the nations "conspire" against the Lord while the second- to third-century-BC Septuagint Greek translation of Psalm 2 used a more powerful word for opposition by saying that the nations "rage" against the Lord. On the other hand, in Psalm 2:7–8 above, the Davidic king might inherit the nations. Likewise, the psalmist taught about nations going from opposing the Lord to belonging to the Lord.

Psalm 22:27–29

> ²⁷ All the ends of the earth
> will remember and turn to the LORD,
> and all the families of the nations
> will bow down before him,
> ²⁸ for dominion belongs to the LORD
> and he rules over the nations.
>
> ²⁹ All the rich of the earth will feast and worship;
> all who go down to the dust will kneel before him—
> those who cannot keep themselves alive.
> (Psalm 22:27–29)

Psalm 22:27–29 proclaims that all people from all nations will bow before the Lord while 22:28 said that the Lord already rules over the nations. On one hand, the Lord already rules over the nations while the nations rage against him. On the other hand, the nations will eventually cease to rage against the Lord and bow before the Lord.

Psalm 86:9

⁹ All the nations you have made
will come and worship before you, Lord;
they will bring glory to your name.
(Psalm 86:9)

Psalm 86:9, similar to Psalm 22:27-29 above, proclaims that all nations will eventually worship the Lord. The nations exist with a purpose of worshiping and glorifying the Lord.

Psalm 102:15–16

¹⁵ The nations will fear the name of the LORD,
all the kings of the earth will revere your glory.
¹⁶ For the LORD will rebuild Zion
and appear in his glory.
(Psalm 102:15–16)

Psalm 102:15–16 proclaimed the nations and the kings of the earth would revere the Lord. The psalmist taught that the future reverence of the nations and kings of the earth tied into the Lord rebuilding Zion and the Lord appearing to people. And the word *Zion* refers to the city of Jerusalem. Likewise, the psalmist proclaimed that the Lord would rebuild Jerusalem and gloriously appear to the nations and kings of the earth.

Psalm 110

¹ The LORD says to my lord:
"Sit at my right hand
until I make your enemies
a footstool for your feet."
² The LORD will extend your mighty scepter from Zion, saying,
"Rule in the midst of your enemies!"
(Psalm 110:1–2)

> ⁵ The Lord is at your right hand;
> he will crush kings on the day of his wrath.
> ⁶ He will judge the nations, heaping up the dead
> and crushing the rulers of the whole earth.
> (Psalm 110:5–6)

Psalm 110 looks like a Davidic coronation Psalm, similar to Psalm 2 earlier in this chapter. And Jesus identified himself with the Davidic king in Psalm 110:1 while the prophecy of this Psalm finds complete fulfillment only in Christ.[11]

The Psalm proclaims the Lord's empowerment of the Davidic king to defeat his enemies. And verses 110:5–6 describes large-scale judgment and wrath against kings and nations—for example, "heaping up the dead."

Summary

The Psalms present paradoxical views of the nations and their kings: (1) the nations rage against the Lord; (2) the Lord currently rules over the nations; (3) a Davidic king may inherit the nations; (4) the Lord would judge and punish the nations; (5) the nations would revere and worship the Lord. And all of these views of the nations continue to develop in end-time prophecy.

---

11. See Matthew 22:41–45, Mark 12:35–37, and Luke 20:41–44.

5

Isaiah

THE BOOK OF ISAIAH addresses many important issues related to judgment, messianic prophecy, and end-time prophecy. The first verse of Isaiah says that the prophet Isaiah saw visions during the reigns of Uzziah, Jotham, Ahaz, and Hezekiah, kings of Judah in the eighth century BC. However, various chapters of the book of Isaiah look like writings from the perspective of the Babylonian exile in the sixth century BC. The exilic perspectives led to various criticisms of multiple authorship/editorship of the book of Isaiah. Regardless of these details of authorship and editorship, the messages of judgment, messianic prophecy, and end-time prophecy remain mostly the same, which this chaper reviews in selections from Isaiah.

ISAIAH 1

Isaiah 1 rebuked the corruption and rebellion of the Israelites while pronouncing judgment and calling them to repentance. For instance, Isaiah 1:7–8 said that the they suffered violent raids from foreigners because the Israelites disobeyed the Lord. And 1:10 compared the rulers and people of Judah to the wicked cities of Sodom and Gomorrah.[1]

Isaiah 1:11–20 revealed the Lord's disgust with religious ceremonies performed by wicked people while calling the wicked people to repentance. The Lord in 1:18 offered forgiveness and cleansing of sins. And verse 1:19 taught that the condition of obedience to the Lord ensured the best crops and livestock while 1:20 taught that the condition of continued rebellion to the Lord ensured destruction by the sword.

---

1. See Sodom and Gomorrah in Genesis 18:16—19:29.

Isaiah 1:21–29 revealed a slice of life in eighth-century-BC Judah. Many people committed murder; rulers took bribes; few people defended the fatherless and widows; many people worshiped polytheistic deity in the shade of so-called sacred oak trees. All of these sins violated covenantal conditions that resulted in divine judgment. Likewise, verse 1:31 taught that disobedient people and their work would burn from an unquenchable fire.

ISAIAH 2:1–5

The dark disobedience and judgment in Isaiah 1 preceded the great light in Isaiah 2:1–5:

> [1] This is what Isaiah son of Amoz saw concerning Judah and Jerusalem:
> [2] In the last days
> the mountain of the LORD's temple will be established
> as the highest of the mountains;
> it will be exalted above the hills,
> and all nations will stream to it.
> [3] Many peoples will come and say,
> "Come, let us go up to the mountain of the LORD,
> to the temple of the God of Jacob.
> He will teach us his ways,
> so that we may walk in his paths."
> The law will go out from Zion,
> the word of the LORD from Jerusalem.
> [4] He will judge between the nations
> and will settle disputes for many peoples.
> They will beat their swords into plowshares
> and their spears into pruning hooks.
> Nation will not take up sword against nation,
> nor will they train for war anymore.
> [5] Come, descendants of Jacob,
> let us walk in the light of the LORD.
> (Isaiah 2:1–5)

Isaiah 2:1-5 presents a glorious picture of the messianic age. The nations stream to the Lord while wars between nations cease—world peace.

The Isaiah 2:2 phrase *in the last days,* an important biblical motif, refers to the end times. And the phrase *the mountain of the Lord's temple* refers to Mount Moria in Jerasulem where Solomon built his temple while Mount Moria currently contains the Western/Wailing Wall remains from the Second Temple and the Islamic Dome of the Rock.[2]

Isaiah 2:3 says that the word of the Lord would go out from Jerusalem. Similarly, Jesus said that preaching the gospel would spread to all nations while beginning in Jerusalem.[3] And 2:4 declares eventual world peace. On one hand, history indicates that the gospel of Christ began in Jerusalem and spread to many nations. On the other hand, history indicates nothing remotely close to world peace. This paradox of prophetic fulfillment works in the context of Christ inaugurating the messianic age during his first-century ministry and Christ consumating the messianic age during his future return.[4] And the 2:1–5 passage by itself might not suggest two major phases in the messianic age while contrasting prophecy in Isaiah 52:13—53:12 of a suffering priestly Messiah and Isaiah 9:6-7 of a triumphant Davidic Messiah suggest different phases.[5]

ISAIAH 4:2-6

> [2] In that day the Branch of the LORD will be beautiful and glorious, and the fruit of the land will be the pride and glory of the survivors in Israel. [3] Those who are left in Zion, who remain in Jerusalem, will be called holy, all who are recorded among the living in Jerusalem. [4] The Lord will wash away the filth of the women of Zion; he will cleanse the bloodstains from Jerusalem by a spirit of judgment and a spirit of fire. [5] Then the LORD will create over all of Mount Zion and over those who assemble there a cloud of smoke by day and a glow of flaming fire by night; over everything the glory will be a canopy. [6] It will be a shelter and shade from the heat of the day, and a refuge and hiding place from the storm and rain. (Isaiah 4:2-6)

2. Nebuchadnezzar in 586 BC destroyed Solomon's Temple (2 Chronicles 36:15-19); Israelites in 538 BC returned from exile to Jerusalem to rebuild the temple according to the decree of Cyrus of Persia, and the Israelites in 515 BC finished rebuilding the temple (Ezra 1:1—6:18); Herod in 19 BC began to expand the temple; Titus in AD 70 destroyed the expanded temple except for the retaining walls including the Western/Wailing Wall; Muslims in AD 691 completed the Dome of the Rock.

3. See Luke 24:46-47.

4. See chapters 1 and 10.

5. Jewish tradition rejects that Isaiah 52:13—53:12 teaches about a suffering Messiah while Jewish tradition says that the suffering servant in these verses symbolically represents the nation of Israel.

Isaiah 4:2–6 presented imagery of judgment followed by the messianic age. These verses declared that the Israelite survivors of divine judgment would prosper. The Lord would use a spirit of judgment and fire to make the Israelite survivors holy (set apart for the Lord) and cleansed from sin. Also, the Lord would create over Mount Zion/Moria in Jerusalem a canopy cloud of smoke by day and a flaming fire by night. This canopy would shelter believers from the Near Eastern heat and rain.

The imagery of the cloud of smoke by day and the flaming fire by night is reminiscent of the Israelites' forty-year journey in the desert after the exodus from slavery in Egypt. During these desert years, the Lord guided and protected the Israelites with a pillar of cloud by day and gave them light with a pillar of fire by night.[6] These pillars represented the glorious presence and protection of the Lord while the Lord led the Israelites to the land of Canaan promised to Abraham.[7] Likewise, Isaiah took this glorious imagery of divine clouds and fire from second-millennium BC history and projected the imagery into the messianic age. Also, Isaiah 4:2–6 indicates a pattern of divine judgment followed by divine blessing.

ISAIAH 9:6–7

> [6] For to us a child is born,
> to us a son is given,
> and the government will be on his shoulders.
> And he will be called
> Wonderful Counselor, Mighty God,
> Everlasting Father, Prince of Peace.
> [7] Of the greatness of his government and peace
> there will be no end.
> He will reign on David's throne
> and over his kingdom,
> establishing and upholding it
> with justice and righteousness
> from that time on and forever.
> The zeal of the LORD Almighty
> will accomplish this.
> (Isaiah 9:6–7)

---

6. See Exodus 13:21—40:38, Leviticus 16:2, and Numbers 9:15—16:42.

7. See chapter 3.

This famous Christmas passage declared the eventual birth of the Davidic Messiah. His righteous government and peace would never end.

In some sense, this messianic prophecy included the conditions of the Davidic dynasty. For example, the prophecy of the Messiah's success depended on his faithfulness. Fortunately, the Messiah ended up the incorruptible God Almighty birthed as a human.[8] And the Messiah would never lack faithfulness and always fulfill his divine destiny.

ISAIAH 11

Isaiah 11:1–5, similar to 9:6–7 above, declared the birth and success of the Davidic Messiah. For instance, 11:1 said, "A shoot will come up from the stump of Jesse" while Jesse fathered David.[9]

Isaiah 11:6–9 follows by presenting powerful imagery of peace in the messianic age:

> [6] The wolf will live with the lamb,
> the leopard will lie down with the goat,
> the calf and the lion and the yearling together;
> and a little child will lead them.
> [7] The cow will feed with the bear,
> their young will lie down together,
> and the lion will eat straw like the ox.
> [8] The infant will play near the cobra's den,
> the young child will put its hand into the viper's nest.
> [9] They will neither harm nor destroy
> on all my holy mountain,
> for the earth will be filled with the knowledge of the LORD
> as the waters cover the sea.
> (Isaiah 11:6–9)

Isaiah 11:6–9 used utopian symbolism to describe peace in the messianic age: wolves live with lambs; leopards lie down with goats; calves dwell with lions, infants safely play near cobras and vipers; nobody causes harm or destruction while knowledge of the Lord floods the earth. The Lord offers utopian peace in the messianic age to those who keep to the conditions of the Lord's covenant. The Lord offers utopian peace in the messianic age to those who keep to the conditions of the Lord's covenant.

---

8. See John 1:1–14, Colossians 1:15–20, and Hebrews 1.
9. See 1 Samuel 16:1–13.

ISAIAH 13:1—14:27

Isaiah 13-23 compiled prophecy that pronounced judgments against eighth-century BC Near Eastern nations while 13:1—14:27 focused on the capital city of Babylon. The fulfillment of the prophecy against Babylon occurred in 689 BC when Assyria sacked Babylon. Also, Isaiah 23:13 specifically said that the Assyrians turned the fortresses of the Babylonians into ruins, which referred to the same sack of Babylon. However, possibly a secondary fulfillment of the prophecy occurred in 539 when Persia overthrew Babylon. The latter developed into an end-time prophetic symbol representing the destruction of governmental forces that violently oppose the people of God.[10] The prophecy against Babylon in 13:1—14:27 included the Lord commanding a destructive attack against Babylon, descriptions or terror and destruction, pronouncement of judgment against sins, prediction of the restoration of Israel, and a lengthy taunt against the king of Babylon.

For instance, Isaiah 13:19-20 pronounced the destruction of Babylon:

> [19] Babylon, the jewel of kingdoms,
> the pride and glory of the Babylonians,
> will be overthrown by God
> like Sodom and Gomorrah.
> [20] She will never be inhabited
> or lived in through all generations;
> there no nomads will pitch their tents,
> there no shepherds will rest their flocks.
> (Isaiah 13:19-20)

The Isaiah 13:19-20 pronouncement of inhabitants ceasing to live for all generations in the capital city of Babylon appears hyperbolic. Babylon rose again within decades after the respective 689 BC Assyrian sack. In 626, Babylon successfully revolted against Assyria. Then, in 612, Babylon overthrew the Assyrian Empire. Babylon also remained inhabited until the third or second century BC. After that, the prophecy stood literally true for nearly two millennia. For example, various people built neighboring cities in what is now the Province of Babil, Iraq, while no city ever reappeared over the ruins of Babylon. However, archeologists inhabited the land in nineteenth and twentieth centuries AD. In the

---

10. See chapters 12 and 14.

1980s, former Iraqi president Saddam Hussein refurbished some ancient Babylonian buildings and used 2,500-year-old Babylonian bricks to build an elaborate palace and vacationed in it. Since the fall of Hussein, visitors to the land of Babylon included military occupants and tourists such as honeymooners staying in the elaborate Hussein suite.[11]

Isaiah 14:3–23 taunted the king of Babylon. For instance, Isaiah 14:9–11 pronounced suffering torment in the king's afterlife:

> [9] The realm of the dead below is all astir
>   to meet you at your coming;
> it rouses the spirits of the departed to greet you—
>   all those who were leaders in the world;
> it makes them rise from their thrones—
>   all those who were kings over the nations.
> [10] They will all respond,
>   they will say to you,
> "You also have become weak, as we are;
>   you have become like us."
> [11] All your pomp has been brought down to the grave,
>   along with the noise of your harps;
> maggots are spread out beneath you
>   and worms cover you.
> (Isaiah 14:9–11)

Isaiah 14:9–11 might be the earliest written biblical passage that teaches about sinners suffering after death. The imagery included spirits of departed kings who greet and taunt the departed king of Babylon while he suffers from maggots.

Also, Isaiah 14:12–15 described the king of Babylon while using imagery of a being fallen from heaven:

> [12] How you have fallen from heaven,
>   morning star, son of the dawn!
> You have been cast down to the earth,
>   you who once laid low the nations!
> [13] You said in your heart,
>   "I will ascend to the heavens;
> I will raise my throne
>   above the stars of God;
> I will sit enthroned on the mount of assembly,
>   on the utmost heights of Mount Zaphon.

---

11. See Myers, "Babylon Ruins Reopen," A14.

¹⁴ I will ascend above the tops of the clouds;
   I will make myself like the Most High."
¹⁵ But you are brought down to the realm of the dead,
   to the depths of the pit.
   (Isaiah 14:12–15)

Isaiah 14:12–15 pictured the king of Babylon as attempting to rule above God in heaven while instead falling from heaven into a grave, a pejorative taunt. The king wanted the power of God, but ended dead.

Many claim that these verses also describe the fall of Satan from heaven. For example, the fifth-century-AD Latin Vulgate and the seventeenth-century King James Version translated the word for *O morning star* to *Lucifer* while many people assume from these translations that Satan was named *Lucifer* before Satan fell from heaven. Many also assume that Luke 10:18 refers to Satan's original fall from heaven. Also, this teaching about Lucifer includes that he led worship among angels in heaven before he eventually rebelled while instigating a third of the angels to rebel with him. However, this interpretation has several problems. First, the king of Babylon foreshadowed the final antichrist who differs from Satan.[12] Second, Luke 10:18 referred to Satan falling from the heavenly realms during a mission of seventy-two disciples of Jesus instead of Satan falling from heaven before the fall of humanity. Third, nothing in the Bible suggests that Satan led angels in worship before he rebelled against the Lord. For instance, Job 38:6–7 used imagery of angels singing and shouting in response to the Lord creating the earth while nothing in the Bible suggested that Lucifer led the singing. Regardless of this controversy, the prophetic imagery in Isaiah 14:12–15 and the rest of 13:1—14:27 initally prophesied about seventh-century-BC events and foreshadowed prophecy about the antichrist and his government in the end times, which this book explores in chapters 12 and 14.

ISAIAH 19

Isaiah 19:1–17 pronounced judgment and wrath against the nation of Egypt while 19:18–25 declared that after the judgment, Egypt would turn to the Lord along with Assyria and Israel. For example, Isaiah 19:22–25:

---

12. See chapter 14.

> ²² The LORD will strike Egypt with a plague; he will strike them and heal them. They will turn to the LORD, and he will respond to their pleas and heal them.
> ²³ In that day there will be a highway from Egypt to Assyria. The Assyrians will go to Egypt and the Egyptians to Assyria. The Egyptians and Assyrians will worship together. ²⁴ In that day Israel will be the third, along with Egypt and Assyria, a blessing on the earth. ²⁵ The LORD Almighty will bless them, saying, "Blessed be Egypt my people, Assyria my handiwork, and Israel my inheritance." (Isaiah 19:22–25)

Isaiah 19:22 prophesied that the Lord would strike wrath against Egypt and then heal Egypt. Then, Egypt would turn to the Lord. This, similar to 4:2–6, indicates a pattern of divine judgment followed by divine restoration.

The next verses, Isaiah 19:23–25, prophesied about Egypt, Assyria, and Israel turning to the Lord. This looked amazing because Egypt and Assyria were two of the most prominent enemies of Israel. For instance, Assyria dominated the Near East during most of the ninth to seventh centuries BC while frequently raiding the Israelites. Isaiah rebuked Assyria in Isaiah 10:5–19, 14:24–27, 30:31, and 31:8–9. Also, Assyria ruled over the land of Babylon during most of this time while apart from different historical periods the land of the Assyrians and the land of the Babylonians are mostly synonymous—the land of Mesopotamia. Likewise, this prophecy implied that Egypt, Assyria/Babylonia, and Israel would turn to the Lord.

Nothing close to the fulfillment of Isaiah 19:22–25 occurred until ancient church history.[13] For example, on one hand, Egypt suffered wrath from major miltary defeats in 605 BC from Babylon, 525 BC from Persia, 332 BC from Greece, and 30 BC from Rome while none of these defeats directly resulted in Egypt turning to the Lord. On the other hand, in some sense, Rome defeating Egypt helped to set up multitudes of Egyptians turning to the Lord during the expansion of the ancient church while multitudes of people in the lands of Israel and Mesopotamia also turned to the Lord during the expansion of the ancient church. However, Muslims conquered these lands in the seventh century, so the ancient church expansion might not have been the complete fulfillment of the prophecy. And if the ancient church expansion did not completely fulfill

---

13. AD 30 to AD 476.

that prophecy, then (A) the prophecy was conditional and the people of these lands failed to keep to the conditions; or (B) the prophecy will be fulfilled in the future; or (C) both A and B. The cases of B or C could make this an end-time prophecy of Egypt, Israel, and Iraq turning to the Lord. This works with Isaiah 2, which as stated earlier, declared that multitudes from all nations would stream to the Lord.

ISAIAH 40:1–5

> [1] Comfort, comfort my people,
>   says your God.
> [2] Speak tenderly to Jerusalem,
>   and proclaim to her
> that her hard service has been completed,
>   that her sin has been paid for,
> that she has received from the LORD's hand
>   double for all her sins.
>
> [3] A voice of one calling:
> "In the wilderness prepare
>   the way for the LORD;
> make straight in the desert
>   a highway for our God. [4] Every valley shall be raised up,
>   every mountain and hill made low;
> the rough ground shall become level,
>   the rugged places a plain.
> [5] And the glory of the LORD will be revealed,
>   and all people will see it together.
> For the mouth of the LORD has spoken."
> (Isaiah 40:1–5)

Isaiah 40:1–5, similar to 4:2–6 and 19, indicates a pattern of divine judgment and wrath followed by restoration. Then, verses 40:3–5 prophesied about both the postexilic restoration of Jerusalem and the messianic age. For instance, Isaiah 40:1–2 proclaimed the end of punishments suffered by the exiled Israelites from Jerusalem and the kingdom of Judah, which occurred when Cyrus of Persia in 539–538 BC overthrew Babylon and declared that exiled Israelites should return to Jerusalem with abundant supplies to build a temple for the Lord.[14] And verses 40:3–5 describes a prophet making preparations for the revelation

---

14. See 2 Chronicles 36:22–23 and Ezra 1:1–4.

of the Lord. On one hand, postexilic prophets fulfilled this prophecy by helping with the sixth-century-BC restoration of Jerusalem. On the other hand, John the Baptist in the first century AD fulfilled this prophecy while he declared the coming of the Messiah.[15] In sum, these verses declared judgment and wrath eventually followed by the blessings of restoration and the messianic age.

ISAIAH 45:22–25

> [22] "Turn to me and be saved,
>   all you ends of the earth;
>   for I am God, and there is no other.
> [23] By myself I have sworn,
>   my mouth has uttered in all integrity
>   a word that will not be revoked:
> Before me every knee will bow;
>   by me every tongue will swear.
> [24] They will say of me, 'In the LORD alone
>   are deliverance and strength.'"
> All who have raged against him
>   will come to him and be put to shame.
> [25] But all the descendants of Israel
>   will find deliverance in the LORD
>   and will make their boast in him.
> (Isaiah 45:22–25)

The Lord in Isaiah 45:22 called all people on earth to turn to him for salvation while the Lord proclaimed monotheism. And 45:23–24 prophesied the destiny of all people eventually bowing to the Lord and swearing, "In the Lord alone are righteousness and strength." And all who rage against the Lord eventually suffer shame. And 45:25 prophesied that eventually all Israelites would be righteous.

This prophetic paradox on one hand taught that all people would swear allegiance to the Lord and likewise all Israelites would be righteous while on the other hand taught that all who rage against the Lord would suffer shame. And history indicates that many Israelites and non-Israelites raged against the Lord.

---

15. See Matthew 3, Mark 1:1–8, and Luke 3:1–18.

ISAIAH 46–47

Isaiah 46–47 prophesied the overthrow of Babylon that would end the Babylonian exile of the Israelites. As stated earlier, the fulfillment of this prophecy occurred in 539–538 BC when Cyrus of Persia overthrew Babylon and decreed that Israelites could restore Jerusalem. Also, as stated earlier, the overthrow of Babylon developed into an end-time prophetic symbol representing the destruction of governmental forces that violently oppose the people of God.

ISAIAH 60:1–3

> [1] Arise, shine, for your light has come,
>   and the glory of the LORD rises upon you.
> [2] See, darkness covers the earth
>   and thick darkness is over the peoples,
> but the LORD rises upon you
>   and his glory appears over you.
> [3] Nations will come to your light,
>   and kings to the brightness of your dawn.
> (Isaiah 60:1–3)

These inspirational verses proclaimed a special presence of the Lord. The light and glory of the Lord floods the believer. The believer struggles between darkness covering the earth and the glorious presence of the Lord, which typifies the first major phase of the messianic age. The nations and kings would come to the light of the Lord, which agrees with "The Nations and Kings in Psalms" in chapter 4 and Isaiah 2.

ISAIAH 65

Isaiah 65 repeats the pattern in 4:2–6, 19, and 40:1–5 of judgment followed by the blessings of the messianic age. The Lord in Isaiah 65:1–16 reminisced about continually revealing himself to obstinate people while pronouncing judgment and the eventual restoration of Judah. Then, verses 65:17–25 springs into images of the messianic age. The verses speak of (1) new heavens and a new earth, (2) the end of weeping and crying, (3) no infant deaths and all good people living over 100 years, (4) everybody building a house for themselves instead of for others, (5) no hard work in vain, (6) no children doomed to misfortune, (7) everybody blessed by the Lord, (8) the Lord answering before people finish asking,

(9) a wolf and lamb feeding together, and (10) a lion eating straw instead of other mammals. Also, the serpent that tempted Eve eats only dust representing death while nobody harms or destroys the people of the Lord.

ISAIAH 66:22–24

> [22] "As the new heavens and the new earth that I make will endure before me," declares the LORD, "so will your name and descendants endure. [23] From one New Moon to another and from one Sabbath to another, all mankind will come and bow down before me," says the LORD. [24] "And they will go out and look on the dead bodies of those who rebelled against me; the worms that eat them will not die, the fire that burns them will not be quenched, and they will be loathsome to all mankind." (Isaiah 66:22–24)

The book of Isaiah ends with Isaiah 66:22-24, which includes the following points: (1) The Israelites would endure; (2) the new heavens and the new earth would endure; (3) all humanity would bow before the Lord; (4) those who bow before the Lord would look at the dead bodies of the rebellious; (5) the bodies of the rebellious would exist with worms that never die and unquenchable fire; (6) the bodies of the rebellious would disgust all humanity. Also, some of these points parallel end-time themes examined earlier in this chapter. For example, the endurance of the messianic king also represented the endurance of the Israelites; Isaiah 65 introduced the new heavens and the new earth; Isaiah 45:23 prophesied that the knee of every person would bow before the Lord; Isaiah 45:24 pronounced that all who rage against the Lord would be put to shame; Isaiah 14:11 declared that maggots (worms) would surround the dead king of Babylon; Isaiah 1:31 described divine judgment and wrath as unquenchable fire.

The new heavens and the new earth represent heaven.[16] Conversely, worms that never die and unquenchable fire represent hell.[17]

The images of worms that never die and unquenchable fire developed from the Israelite tradition about the Valley of Ben Hinnom. Some kings of Judah sacrificed their children on polytheistic altars in the Valley of Ben Hinnom, and many other people did the same. Due to

---

16. See Revelation 21–22.
17. See Mark 9:43–48 and Revelation 20:10–15.

eventual Israelite repugnance of the child sacrifice in the Valley of Ben Hinnom, the Israelites turned it into a burning garbage dump while according to legend the fire perpetuated from continuous loads of garbage including the carcasses of animals and humans. Also, flies perpetually laid eggs in the carcasses and other garbage not yet burned and caused a never-ending generation of maggots, which look like worms. The term *Gehenna* derived from the phrase *the Valley of Ben Hinnom*. Eventually, Gehenna with the perpetual generation of maggots and unquenchable fire developed into a symbol for *hell* where sinners suffer punishments in the afterlife.

SUMMARY

Isaiah presented important end-time themes. They included conditions for judgment, punishment with fire, cleansing with fire, judgment and punishment followed by restoration, the Davidic Messiah, and a future utopia.

6

Jeremiah

JEREMIAH STARTED HIS PROPHETIC ministry to the kingdom of Judah around 626 BC.[1] By this time, the Northern Kingdom of Israel had ceased to exist for almost one century while the events of the destruction of the Northern Kingdom foreshadowed the destruction of Judah and its capital Jerusalem. As noted in chapter 4, the Lord allowed the Assyrian Empire to destroy the Northern Kingdom because the northern Israelites disobeyed the Lord by worshiping golden calves and polytheistic deities, practicing divination and sorcery, and sacrificing their children on altars. Also, Hoshea, the last king of the Northern Kingdom, served as a subject king and paid taxes to Assyrian king Shalmaneser. But Hoshea committed treason and Shalmaneser ceased to tolerate the Northern Kingdom while forcing all of the northern Israelites into exile.[2]

Jeremiah prophesied for more than four decades. Major events during his ministry included:

1. King Josiah of Judah in 622 BC began great reforms—for example, abolishing polytheistic altars.
2. King Nabopolassar of Babylonian in 612 BC sacked Nineveh, the capital of the Assyrian Empire, and this military victory inaugurated the Neo-Babylonian Empire.
3. Josiah in 609 BC died in battle against Pharaoh Neco of Egypt.
4. King Jehoahaz succeeded his father Josiah and reverted to polytheism.

---

1. See Jeremiah 1:1–3.
2. See 2 Kings 17.

5. Jehoahaz reigned only three months before Neco imprisoned Jehoahaz.

6. Neco made Jehoiakim, another son of Josiah, the king of Judah and imposed an expensive tax on Judah.

7. Jehoiakim also reverted to polytheism.

8. Babylonian crown prince Nebuchadnezzar in 605 BC defeated Neco in the Battle of Carchemish while taking control of large parts of southwest Asia.

9. Nebuchadnezzar in 604 BC assumed the throne of the Babylonian Empire after the death of his father Nabopolassar.

10. Jehoiakim become a subject king and paid taxes to Nebuchadnezzar for three years, but Jehoiakim changed his mind and rebelled against Nebuchadnezzar.

11. Jehoiachin, the son of Jehoiakim, in 598 BC succeeded his father as the king of Judah.

12. After Jehoiachin reigned three months, Nebuchadnezzar in 597 BC sacked Jerusalem, sent many Israelites into exile, and made Zedekiah, an uncle of Jehoiachin, the king of Judah.

13. Zedekiah rebelled against Nebuchadnezzar, who in 586 BC destroyed Jerusalem and sent many more Israelites into exile.[3]

HIGHLIGHTS OF JEREMIAH

Highlights in the ministry of Jeremiah included the following points: (1) Jeremiah rebuked the Israelites for stealing, murdering, committing adultery, perjury, worshiping other gods, and child sacrifice;[4] (2) Jeremiah taught about the conditional dynamics of predictive prophecy;[5] (3) Jeremiah prophetically predicted the Babylonian exile and warned that the Israelites and other nations would endure if they accepted the punishment from Babylon or they would suffer destruction if they resisted the punishment from Babylon;[6] (4) Jeremiah prophesied about

---

3. See 2 Kings 22:1—25:21.

4. See Jeremiah 7. These rebukes look similar to Isaiah's rebukes according to chapter 5

5. See chapter 1.

6. See Jeremiah 27.

the restoration of Israel and the messianic age;[7] (5) Jeremiah announced the downfall of various nations.[8] The next three sections in this chapter focus on points three to five.

ENDURE OR SUFFER DESTRUCTION

> [1] Early in the reign of Zedekiah son of Josiah king of Judah, this word came to Jeremiah from the LORD: [2] This is what the LORD said to me: "Make a yoke out of straps and crossbars and put it on your neck. [3] Then send word to the kings of Edom, Moab, Ammon, Tyre and Sidon through the envoys who have come to Jerusalem to Zedekiah king of Judah. [4] Give them a message for their masters and say, 'This is what the LORD Almighty, the God of Israel, says: "Tell this to your masters: [5] With my great power and outstretched arm I made the earth and its people and the animals that are on it, and I give it to anyone I please. [6] Now I will give all your countries into the hands of my servant Nebuchadnezzar king of Babylon; I will make even the wild animals subject to him. [7] All nations will serve him and his son and his grandson until the time for his land comes; then many nations and great kings will subjugate him.
>
> [8] "'If, however, any nation or kingdom will not serve Nebuchadnezzar king of Babylon or bow its neck under his yoke, I will punish that nation with the sword, famine and plague, declares the LORD, until I destroy it by his hand. [9] So do not listen to your prophets, your diviners, your interpreters of dreams, your mediums or your sorcerers who tell you, 'You will not serve the king of Babylon.' [10] They prophesy lies to you that will only serve to remove you far from your lands; I will banish you and you will perish. [11] But if any nation will bow its neck under the yoke of the king of Babylon and serve him, I will let that nation remain in its own land to till it and to live there, declares the LORD.""'" (Jeremiah 27:1–11)

The Lord in these verses told Jeremiah to send messages to the nearby kings of Edom, Moab, Ammon, Tyre, and Sidon. The Lord pronounced that he would give all of these nations to Babylonian king Nebuchadnezzar. On one hand, the people from these nations would endure if they would surrender to the Lord's judgment and punishment by subjecting themselves to the king of Babylon. On the other hand, these nations

---

7. See Jeremiah 29–33.
8. See Jeremiah 46–51.

would suffer destruction if they would try to fight against the king of Babylon. Also, Jeremiah 27:12–15 said that the same options applied to Judah. The Israelites could accept the judgment from the Lord and surrender to the king of Babylon while enduring in Judah or they could rebel against the king of Babylon while suffering destruction. Resistance was futile.

These verses teach about conditions in divine judgment. Chronic rebellion against the Lord from the nations of Judah, Edom, Moab, Ammon, Tyre, and Sidon led to the point of inevitable judgment while conditions permitted the endurance of these nations. Also, the Lord planned for the Israelites to prosper in the Babylonian Empire according to Jeremiah 29:4–7:

> ⁴ This is what the LORD Almighty, the God of Israel, says to all those I carried into exile from Jerusalem to Babylon: ⁵ "Build houses and settle down; plant gardens and eat what they produce. ⁶ Marry and have sons and daughters; find wives for your sons and give your daughters in marriage, so that they too may have sons and daughters. Increase in number there; do not decrease. ⁷ Also, seek the peace and prosperity of the city to which I have carried you into exile. Pray to the LORD for it, because if it prospers, you too will prosper." (Jeremiah 29:4–7)

The Lord in these verses planned for more than the endurance of the exiled Israelites. The Lord planned for their prosperity. Also, the conditional options of endurance or suffering destruction described earlier had developed into conditional options of prosperity or destruction. Unfortunately, King Zedekiah and most people in his kingdom chose destruction. However, some Israelites chose prosperity and the Lord declared a model of prospering from judgment and punishment.

RESTORATION AFTER JUDGMENT

According to Jeremiah 25:1–14, when Babylonian Crown Prince Nebuchadnezzar defeated Egyptian Pharaoh Neco in the Battle of Carchemish in 605 BC, Jeremiah prophesied that the people of Judah and neighboring nations would serve the king of Babylon for seventy years and then Babylon would cease to exist. Sixty-seven years later in 538 BC, Cyrus of Persia destroyed Babylon. The next year, Cyrus decreed that Israelites should return to Jerusalem to rebuild its temple, which ended the Babylonian exile. Also, the inexact number of sixty-seven years rounded to seventy years while the overthrow of Babylon fulfilled the prophecy. Additionally, Zechariah 1:12–17 implied a secondary fulfillment of the seventy years occurred from 586 BC to 515 BC. In this case, Nebuchadnezzar destroyed the Jerusalem temple in 586 BC and the postexilic Israelites finished rebuilding the temple in 515 BC.[9] Likewise, the overthrow of Babylon paved the way for the postexilic restoration of Jerusalem. For example, Jeremiah 30:3:

> "'The days are coming,' declares the LORD, 'when I will bring my people Israel and Judah back from captivity and restore them to the land I gave their ancestors to possess,' says the LORD." (Jeremiah 30:3)

The Lord first began to fulfill the Jeremiah 30:3 prophecy in 538 BC when Cyrus, as noted earlier, declared that exiled Israelites should return to Jerusalem with abundant supplies to build a temple for the Lord. Also, the Lord planned more than restoration but a new covenant according to Jeremiah 31:31–34:

> [31] "The days are coming," declares the LORD,
>   "when I will make a new covenant
> with the people of Israel
>   and with the people of Judah.
> [32] It will not be like the covenant
> I made with their ancestors
> when I took them by the hand
>   to lead them out of Egypt,
> because they broke my covenant,
>   though I was a husband to them,"
> declares the LORD.
> [33] "This is the covenant I will make with the people of Israel
>   after that time," declares the LORD.
> "I will put my law in their minds
>   and write it on their hearts.
> I will be their God,
>   and they will be my people.
> [34] No longer will they teach their neighbor,
>   or say to one another, 'Know the LORD,'
> because they will all know me,
>   from the least of them to the greatest,"
>   declares the LORD.
> "For I will forgive their wickedness
>   and will remember their sins no more."
> (Jeremiah 31:31–34)

---

9. See Ezra 6.

Jeremiah 31:31–34 prophesied about a new covenant, and the letter to Hebrews identified this new covenant as the Christian covenant. Also, verse 31:32 referred to the Mosiac Covenant, which built upon the Abrahamic Covenant.[10] The Mosaic Covenant included hundreds of laws that required apparently endless hours to memorize. And prophets such as Isaiah and Jeremiah frequently rebuked the Israelites for breaking those laws. However, verses 31:32–34 said that the new covenant would not be like the broken Mosaic Covenant while the Lord would put the laws of the new covenant in the hearts and minds of the Israelites. Moreover, verse 31:34 went as far as saying that in the new covenant nobody would have to teach his neighbor.

The New Testament clearly taught that the new covenant involved believers enjoying a relationship with the Lord who personally speaks to the heart and mind of each believer.[11] This parallels Jeremiah 31:33 prophesying that the Lord would put his new law in the hearts and minds of the Israelites. And a literal interpretation of the imagery in 31:34 describes a time when everybody would know the Lord and nobody would need an evangelist or a biblical teacher. Perhaps this description involved hyperbole or this would find literal fulfillment in the new covenant after the consummation of the messianic age.[12] And the new covenant required the condition of faith, which this book discusses in chapter.

JUDGMENT OF NATIONS

Jeremiah 46–51 pronounced judgment from the Lord to various Near Eastern nations such as Egypt and Babylon. And these judgments were subject to conditions according to Jeremiah 18:1–10, as explained in chapter 1. For instance, Jeremiah 46:14 said to announce the judgment to Egypt, which implied conditions.

---

10. See chapter 3 for the Mosaic Covenant and Abrahamic Covenant.
11. See John 14:26 and Romans 8:16.
12. See chapters 1 and 5.

7

Prince Gog from the Land of Magog

THE BOOK OF EZEKIEL includes various end-time prophecies. This chapter focuses on Ezekiel 38–39, a prophecy against Prince Gog from the land of Magog. The prophecy in 38–39 presumably originated in the sixth century BC after Babylonian king Nebuchadnezzar sent Ezekiel into Babylonian exile. Also, the book of Revelation refers to Ezekiel's prophecy against Gog.

Ezekiel 38–39 prophesied against "Gog, of the land of Magog, the chief prince of Meshek and Tubal." The sixth-century-BC Meshech and Tubal most likely existed within the land of modern day Turkey or Georgia.[1] The word *Magog* most likely means "the land of Gog." Nobody has decisively identified Prince Gog. Perhaps Ezekiel intentionally veiled the identity of Gog because the prophetic events would take place at least decades into the future after the postexilic restoration of Israel. Also, the events evidently have yet to take place roughly 2,600 years later.

---

1. Turkey and Georgia border each other while both are located on the juncture of eastern Europe and western Asia. Turkey is on the east northern border of the Mediterranean Sea while Georgia is on a northern border of Turkey. Also, some Bible translations such as the American Standard Version say that Gog was "the prince of Rosh, Meshech, and Tubal." Debate involves the biblical Hebrew word *rosh*, which means "head" or "chief." For example, the New International Version says that Gog was "the chief prince of Meshech and Tubal," which translated the Hebrew word *rosh* to "chief" while the American Standard Version left *rosh* untranslated and made it one of the nations ruled by Gog. Additionally, some modern writers associate the Hebrew word *rosh* with "Russia" while no evidence from ancient history suggested that *rosh* referred to "Russia." Furthermore, Genesis 10:2 lists the names Magog, Meshech, and Tubal as sons of Japheth.

CONTENT OF EZEKIEL 38-39

In Ezekiel 38:1-6, the word of the Lord came to Ezekiel and told him to prophesy against Prince Gog from the land of Magog. The Lord said that he opposes Gog and would turn Gog around as with a hook in his mouth. Under the control of the Lord, Gog would lead his entire armed forces that ride horses. Also, armies from many nations north of Israel would join Gog in a military coalition.

In Ezekiel 38:7-16, the Lord said for Gog to get ready to command his hordes of coalition troops in the future. His army would advance against Israel after many Israelites returned to Israel from exile. Before the military advance, the postexilic Israelites would eventually live at peace without expecting war. For example, Ezekiel used imagery of Israelites "living without walls and without gates and bars" to emphasize that the restored Israel eventually expected no predatory military attacks. Then, Gog would notice the prosperity of Israel and lead troops from the north to attack and plunder Israel.

In Ezekiel 38:17-23, when Gog and his armies would plan to attack Israel, then the Lord would use miracles of nature to oppose the military forces of Gog. The Lord would send a great earthquake, plague, and torrents of rain, hailstones, and burning sulfur to fight against the troops. Also, troops within Gog's coalition would turn and attack each other. Many nations would see the greatness of the Lord while the Lord defends Israel against its enemies.

In Ezekiel 39:1-6, the Lord repeated that he opposes Gog and would control him while he advances to attack Israel. The Lord would strike and kill Gog and his coalition troops. The Lord would also send fire to the land of Magog.

In Ezekiel 39:7-8, the Lord said that these events would make his name known in Israel and the nations. And the Lord said that this day would surely happen.

In Ezekiel 39:9-10, the Lord said that the Israelites would loot the dead coalition troops. For instance, the Israelites would gather the weapons from the troops while the Israelites would use the material of those weapons for seven years of fuel.

In Ezekiel 39:11-20, the Lord would give Gog and his armies a burial place in Israel. It would take seven months for the Israelites to bury the dead. Also, the Lord used imagery of calling birds and wild animals to feast on the dead troops while he compared the dead troops to a sacrifice.

In Ezekiel 39:21–24, the Lord said that he would display his glory among the nations while all nations see the infliction on those who attacked Israel. After these events, Israel would profoundly know the Lord. All nations would understand that the Israelites previously went into exile because of their sin.

Finally, in Ezekiel 39:25–29, the Lord concluded the prophecy by declaring again that the Israelites contemporary to Ezekiel in Babylonian exile would return to Israel. And the Lord would pour out his Spirit on the people of Israel.

EZEKIEL 38–39 AND MESSIANIC PROPHECY

Ezekiel 38–39 might indicate that Gog's attack against Israel would occur during the messianic age. For example, Ezekiel 38:7–16 described a time when Israel would live in utopian peace with no expectation of war. And such utopian peace never occurred in Israel. Likewise, either Ezekiel figuratively described the peace in Israel or he taught about Israel in the messianic age when Israelites would stop owning weapons of war, which parallels messianic prophecy in Isaiah.[2]

Despite Ezekiel's imagery of Israel reaching utopian peace, wicked people could still arise to plan harm. However, the Israelites would need no military weapons while the Lord would miraculously protect them.

Also, the imagery of Gog and his hordes suffering destruction coincides with imagery from Psalm 110, Ezekiel 39:11–20, and Isaiah 66:22–24. Psalm 110 is messianic prophecy while 110:6 said that the Lord would "judge the nations, heaping up the dead." Ezekiel 39:11–20 said that the Israelites would need seven months to bury the dead troops, which implied a previous "heaping up the dead." And Isaiah 66:24 said that all who bow down to the Lord in the messianic age would "go out and look on the dead bodies of those who rebelled" while Ezekiel 39:9–10 said that the Israelites would go out and not only look at those who rebelled but also loot the dead troops.

---

2. See chapter 5.

EZEKIEL 38-39 AND REVELATION

The book of Revelation used imagery from Ezekiel 38-39. Revelation 16:17-21 described the last bowl of wrath during the overthrow of Babylon before the return of the Lord. And that bowl of wrath overthrew Babylon with the most powerful earthquake in the history of earth and huge hailstones that fell from the sky and hit men. These images in Revelation parallel the great earthquake and hailstones in Ezekiel 38:19-22.

Also, Revelation 19:17-18:

> [17] And I saw an angel standing in the sun, who cried in a loud voice to all the birds flying in midair, "Come, gather together for the great supper of God, [18] so that you may eat the flesh of kings, generals, and the mighty, of horses and their riders, and the flesh of all people, free and slave, great and small." (Revelation 19:17-18)

These verses show an angel that gathers birds to feed on dead military leaders and troops who would die in the Battle of Armageddon during the return of the Lord.[3] And these verses resemble Ezekiel 39:17-18:

> [17] "Son of man, this is what the Sovereign LORD says: Call out to every kind of bird and all the wild animals: 'Assemble and come together from all around to the sacrifice I am preparing for you, the great sacrifice on the mountains of Israel. There you will eat flesh and drink blood. [18] You will eat the flesh of mighty men and drink the blood of the princes of the earth as if they were rams and lambs, goats and bulls—all of them fattened animals from Bashan.'" (Ezekiel 39:17-18)

Both Revelation 19:17-18 and Ezekiel 39:17-18 portray birds feasting on dead military leaders and troops after a major battle. This might suggest a relationship between the respective battles.

However, Revelation also refers to Gog and Magog in battle after the return of the Lord and the 1,000-year reign. Revelation 19:11—20:15 teaches about (1) the return of the Lord and the Battle of Armageddon, (2) Satan's banishment into the Abyss/prison for 1,000 years, (3) the resurrection of martyred Christians, (4) the 1,000-year reign of Jesus

---

3. Revelation 16:16 says that the battle during the return of the Lord would organize in a place called *Armageddon* while Revelation 19:11-21 describes the Battle of Armageddon.

Christ and the resurrected believers, (5) the release of Satan from his prison, (6) Satan gathering multitudes of troops to attack the Lord's people, (7) fire from heaven devouring the satanic troops, and (8) Satan getting thrown into the lake of burning sulfur forever. And Revelation 20:7–10 focuses on the satanic battle after the return of the Lord and the 1,000-year reign:

> [7] When the thousand years are over, Satan will be released from his prison [8] and will go out to deceive the nations in the four corners of the earth—Gog and Magog—and to gather them for battle. In number they are like the sand on the seashore. [9] They marched across the breadth of the earth and surrounded the camp of God's people, the city he loves. But fire came down from heaven and devoured them. [10] And the devil, who deceived them, was thrown into the lake of burning sulfur, where the beast and the false prophet had been thrown. They will be tormented day and night for ever and ever. (Revelation 20:7–10)

Revelation 20:7–10 prophesied that Satan would leave his prison and again deceive the nations in all corners of the earth while gathering them for battle. All the nations are called *Gog and Magog,* an obvious reference to the prophecy in Ezekiel 38–39. However, Ezekiel refers to "Gog" as a chief prince and to "Magog" as Gog's nation while Revelation refers to "Gog and Magog" as the nations of the earth. Regardless of this divergence of word usage, the reference stands. And Satan in Revelation parallels Gog in Ezekiel. Both lead a multitude of troops to attack God's people. And *the city he loves* in Revelation 20:9 referred to Jerusalem, the city that God loves. Likewise, both Satan and Gog would lead multitudes of troops to attack God's people in Jerusalem. Also, the Lord would send a great earthquake, plague, and torrents of rain, hailstones, and burning sulfur to kill Gog's troops while the Lord would send fire to the people in the land of Gog. And the Lord would send fire to devour Satan's troops while the devouring fire in Revelation parallels burning sulfur and fire in Ezekiel.

Revelation drew upon imagery from Ezekiel 38–39 for at least three different scenes: (1) the overthrow of Babylon, (2) the Battle of Armageddon, and (3) the final satanic battle. In some sense, Gog represents the eighth king of the beast (the final antichrist) in the overthrow of Babylon and the Battle of Armageddon while Gog also represents Satan in the final satanic battle. Likewise, interpreters of symbolic end-time prophecy need caution instead of dogmatically asserting a tidy chronology of end-time events because the symbolism might have multiple meanings.

EZEKIEL 38–39 AND CONDITIONAL FUTURISM

Regardless of the literalness or figurativeness of Ezekiel 38–39, conditional futurism proposes that Gog might hear or read this prophecy and repent instead of dying from the wrath of God. Also, various verses in Ezekiel support that the Lord uses all prophetic warnings to wicked people to encourage repentance, while this includes Gog's possible repentance. For instance, according to Ezekiel 3:18, the Lord commanded Ezekiel to persuade wicked people to repent:

> When I say to a wicked person, "You will surely die," and you do not warn them or speak out to dissuade them from their evil ways in order to save their life, that wicked person will die for their sin, and I will hold you accountable for their blood. (Ezekiel 3:18)

This verse near the beginning of the book of Ezekiel explains an important context in Ezekiel's prophetic ministry. The Lord called Ezekiel to warn wicked people about their need to repent. Also, the verse above said that the Lord would hold Ezekiel accountable if he heard a word from the Lord for a wicked person and did not deliver that word to the wicked person.

Also, Ezekiel 18:21–23:

> [21] But if a wicked person turns away from all the sins they have committed and keeps all my decrees and does what is just and right, that person will surely live; they will not die. [22] None of the offenses they have committed will be remembered against them. Because of the righteous things they have done, they will live. [23] Do I take any pleasure in the death of the wicked? declares the Sovereign LORD. Rather, am I not pleased when they turn from their ways and live? (Ezekiel 18:21–23)

Ezekiel 18:21–23 teaches that the Lord always prefers that wicked people repent while the Lord takes no pleasure in the death of the wicked. These verses reveal the heart of the Lord. Despite the divine wrath in various parts of the Bible, God never prefers to send wrath to unrepentant people while he always prefers to send blessings to repentant people.

Also, Ezekiel 33:14–16:

> [14] And if I say to a wicked person, "You will surely die," but they then turn away from their sin and do what is just and right— [15] if they give back what they took in pledge for a loan, return what they have stolen, follow the decrees that give life, and do no evil—that person will surely live; they will not die. [16] None of the sins that person has committed will be remembered against them. They have done what is just and right; they will surely live. (Ezekiel 33:14–16)

These verses taught that when the Lord prophesies the death of a wicked person, then that person could repent of wickedness and live. The condition of repentence is always implicit. Likewise, the prophecy against Gog could persuade Gog to repent of wickedness like attacking utopian Israel.

8

Zechariah

The prophet Zechariah began his postexilic prophetic ministry in 520 BC, the second year of Persian king Darius.[1] Critical events that led up to this time included the following: (1) In 586 BC, Babylonian king Nebuchadnezzar destroyed Judah including the temple in Jerusalem while he exiled all but a few Israelites from Judah; (2) in 538 BC, Cyrus decreed that the Israelites should return to Jerusalem to rebuild the temple for the Lord; (3) in 537 BC, forty thousand Israelites returned to Jerusalem and rebuilt the temple altar for the Lord, resumed biblical sacrifices such as the regular morning and evening sacrifices that ceased in 586 BC, and rebuilt the foundation of the temple; (4) after rebuilding the foundation of the temple in 537 BC, the Israelites faced twenty-two years of opposition before finishing the temple in 515 BC.[2] And Zechariah played an important role in the rebuilding of the temple from 520 BC to 515 BC. For example, Ezra 6:14 said the Israelites in Jerusalem prospered during the preaching of Haggai and Zechariah. And Zechariah 1:7—6:8 compiled eight apocalyptic visions from one night in the first year of his ministry.[3] Also, various scholars reject that Zechariah wrote Zechariah 9–14 while such authorship criticism has no impact on the theological message. This chapter focuses on the role of high priest in Zechariah 3, 4 and 6:9–15 and the end-time prophecy in Zechariah 12–14.

---

1. See Zechariah 1:1.

2. Ezra 1–6 briefly recounts the history from the 537 BC decree of Cyrus to the 515 BC completion of the temple in Jerusalem.

3. As noted in chapter 1, an apocalyptic vision or dream includes important events that involve divine intervention while a divinely appointed mediator helps to interpret the vision.

ZECHARIAH 3

¹ Then he showed me Joshua the high priest standing before the angel of the LORD, and Satan standing at his right side to accuse him. ² The LORD said to Satan, "The LORD rebuke you, Satan! The LORD, who has chosen Jerusalem, rebuke you! Is not this man a burning stick snatched from the fire?"

³ Now Joshua was dressed in filthy clothes as he stood before the angel. ⁴ The angel said to those who were standing before him, "Take off his filthy clothes."

Then he said to Joshua, "See, I have taken away your sin, and I will put fine garments on you."

⁵ Then I said, "Put a clean turban on his head." So they put a clean turban on his head and clothed him, while the angel of the LORD stood by.

⁶ The angel of the LORD gave this charge to Joshua: ⁷ "This is what the LORD Almighty says: 'If you will walk in obedience to me and keep my requirements, then you will govern my house and have charge of my courts, and I will give you a place among these standing here.

⁸ "'Listen, High Priest Joshua, you and your associates seated before you, who are men symbolic of things to come: I am going to bring my servant, the Branch. ⁹ See, the stone I have set in front of Joshua! There are seven eyes on that one stone, and I will engrave an inscription on it,' says the LORD Almighty, 'and I will remove the sin of this land in a single day.

¹⁰ "'In that day each of you will invite your neighbor to sit under your vine and fig tree,' declares the LORD Almighty." (Zechariah 3:1–10)

Zechariah 3 recounted the fourth of eight apocalypses from a single night in 520 BC. Other important background to this apocalypse includes that the Israelites had no anointed high priest since the 586 BC destruction of Jerusalem while Joshua was heir apparent of the postexilic high priesthood.[4] Joshua descended from Aaron, the first Israelite high priest.[5] And Joshua in 536 BC helped to rebuild the Jerusalem temple altar and resumed various biblical sacrifices such as the morning and evening sacrifice, but the Israelites had yet to complete rebuilding the temple when Zechariah saw this vision in 520 BC. Within five years in

---

4. The name *Joshua* is spelled "Jeshua" in the books of Ezra and Nehemiah.
5. See chapter 3.

515 BC, the Israelites finished rebuilding the temple and consecrated Joshua as the high priest.

The apocalypse prophesied about the Lord cleansing Joshua and making him the high priest of the Israelites. Zechariah saw a vision of Joshua wearing filthy clothes while he faced the angel of the Lord. Satan stood at the right side of Joshua while planning to accuse him. Then, the Lord protected Joshua by rebuking Satan. And the angel of the Lord told other angels to remove the filthy clothes from Joshua. The filthy clothes represented sin, the sin of both the high priest and all of the Israelites.[6] Next, Zechariah commanded the angels to put a clean turban on the head of Joshua. And the angels gave Joshua a clean turban and clean clothes. After that, the Lord said that he would make Joshua the governor of the Lord's house if Joshua would follow the Lord and keep his requirements. Likewise, the restoration of the priesthood included conditions.

The Lord also promised Joshua and his priestly associates that "the Branch" would come. As noted in the chapter 5, the biblical term *the Branch* referred to the Davidic Messiah. Likewise, Zechariah's prophecy included the coming Messiah.

ZECHARIAH 4

Zechariah 4, the fifth of eight apocalypses from a single night in 520 BC, symbolically referred to Zerubbabel and Joshua as two olive trees. Cyrus in 536 BC appointed Zerubbabel the governor of Jerusalem while he descended from the Davidic dynasty. Zerubbabel started to rebuild the Jerusalem temple in 536 BC, but as noted earlier, opposition delayed the completion of the temple. And in Zechariah 4, the Lord specifically encouraged Zerubbabel that he would complete rebuilding the temple. This apocalypse portrayed both Zerubbabel and Joshua standing side-by-side as the civil leader and the priestly leader of the Israelites in Jerusalem. The imagery of Zerubbabel and Joshua represented as olive trees symbolized the Lord's anointing on both of them. For instance, olive trees in Jerusalem produced large quantities of olive oil while the Israelites used olive oil to anoint both priests and kings. And anointing represented being chosen and empowered by the Lord.

---

6. In Leviticus 16, the high priest on the Day of Atonement offered sacrifices for the forgiveness of sins for both himself and all of the Israelites.

ZECHARIAH 6:9-15

> ⁹ The word of the LORD came to me: ¹⁰ "Take silver and gold from the exiles Heldai, Tobijah and Jedaiah, who have arrived from Babylon. Go the same day to the house of Josiah son of Zephaniah. ¹¹ Take the silver and gold and make a crown, and set it on the head of the high priest, Joshua son of Jozadak. ¹² Tell him this is what the LORD Almighty says: 'Here is the man whose name is the Branch, and he will branch out from his place and build the temple of the LORD. ¹³ It is he who will build the temple of the LORD, and he will be clothed with majesty and will sit and rule on his throne. And he will be a priest on his throne. And there will be harmony between the two.' ¹⁴ The crown will be given to Heldai, Tobijah, Jedaiah and Hen son of Zephaniah as a memorial in the temple of the LORD. ¹⁵ Those who are far away will come and help to build the temple of the LORD, and you will know that the LORD Almighty has sent me to you. This will happen if you diligently obey the LORD your God." (Zechariah 6:9-15)

Zechariah 6:9-15 occurred after the eight apocalypses in 1:7—6:8. In this prophecy, the Lord directed the prophet Zechariah to visit three exiles who recently moved from Babylon to Jerusalem. Zechariah took gifts of silver and gold from the exiles to make a crown for Joshua the high priest. Verses 6:12-13 jump into a symbolic description of Joshua the high priest that makes Joshua a prefiguration of the Messiah. For example, the Lord said that Joshua's name is "the Branch." And the section on Zechariah 3 said that the Lord promised Joshua that "the Branch" would come while *the Branch* is a biblical term used for the Messiah. Likewise, Zechariah 3 and 6 juxtapose each other by Zechariah 3 distinguishing between Joshua and the Branch and Zechariah 6 identifying Joshua *as* the Branch. And seeing Joshua as a prefiguration of the Messiah helps to make sense of the symbolic puzzle. Also, Zechariah 6:14 said that the crown given to Joshua would display as a memorial in the temple. This implied that Joshua would not keep the crown, which also suggests that he was not the complete messianic Branch but a prefiguration of the Branch.

The final verse of the prophecy encouraged Joshua that more people from far away would help to rebuild the temple. The last sentence of the prophecy clearly taught about the conditions of the prophecy. For instance, Joshua needed to diligently obey the Lord for Joshua to see the fulfillment of the respective prophetic promises.

In sum, Zechariah 3, 4, and 6:9–15 prophesied about the reestablishment and elevation of the Israelite high priesthood while the divine promises to the high priesthood included conditions. Also, chapter 9 discusses how a high priest appeared in the book of Daniel and related to end-time prophecy.

HIGHLIGHTS OF ZECHARIAH 12–14

In Zechariah 12:1–9, the Lord said that nations would surround Jerusalem to attack it, but the Lord would destroy the armies that attempted to attack Jerusalem. Also, the weakest Israelite would be as strong as King David while the house of David would be like God.

Zechariah 12:10–14 prophesied about the piercing of the Lord (YHWH) and the inhabitants of Jerusalem mourning for him.

Zechariah 13 prophesied about a fountain cleansing the house of David and the inhabitants of Jerusalem from sin.

Zechariah 14:1 prophesied about a great plunder while introducing the final attack against Jerusalem.

In Zechariah 14:2, the Lord said that he would gather all nations to attack Jerusalem. The nations would capture the city, ransack the houses, and rape the women. The enemies would send half the people of Jerusalem into exile while the rest remained in the city.

In Zechariah 14:3–5, the Lord appears with his holy ones and they fight against the attacking nations. And the Lord's feet stand on the Mount of Olives in Jerusalem.

In Zechariah 14:9, the Lord becomes king over the entire earth.

In Zechariah 14:11, many people live in Jerusalem and the Lord keeps Jerusalem secure.

Zechariah 14:12–15 described gruesome consequences of those who attacked Jerusalem. When the Lord fights against the attackers of Jerusalem, their flesh rots while they stand on their feet, their eyes rot in their sockets, and their tongues rot in their mouths. And the Lord afflicts the attackers with great panic while they ended up attacking each other.

In Zechariah 14:16–19, the survivors from the nations that attacked Jerusalem go year after year to Jerusalem to worship the King, the Lord Almighty. If any people from any nation avoid going to Jerusalem to worship the Lord, then the Lord plagues them with a drought.

In Zechariah 14:20–21, every common pot and bowl in Jerusalem has an inscription "HOLY TO THE LORD." And no more Canaanites live in the house of the Lord Almighty.

DISCUSSION OF ZECHARIAH 12–14

Zechariah 12–14, presumably written in the fifth century BC, consisted of a single oracle and prophesied about the end times. The major themes of the prophecy included the last attack against Jerusalem, the punishments of Jerusalem's attackers, the security and blessings of Jerusalem in the messianic age, and the conditions for blessings and curses in the messianic age.

Zechariah 12:1–9 and 14:1–15 juxtaposed different details about the attack against Jerusalem. For example, Zechariah 12:1–9 implied that the attackers never penetrated Jerusalem while Zechariah 14:2 said that the attackers initially captured the city, ransacked the houses, raped the women, and sent half the city into exile. This detail in 14:2 makes it difficult to synthesize a literal translation of 14:2 and similar accounts of end-time attacks against Jerusalem in Ezekiel and Revelation, which chapter 7 discussed. However, both Zechariah 14:2 and Ezekiel 38:4 said that the Lord sovereignly organized the opposition against Jerusalem. As noted previously, anybody in the armies opposing Jerusalem could repent and avoid their prophesied judgment. There would be no cases of the Lord sovereignly leading genuinely repentant people into an attack against the Lord's people.

Also, Zechariah 14:3–19 taught about the conditions for blessings and curses in the messianic age. For instance, the Lord stands on the Mount of Olives and reigns as King over the entire earth, a picture of the messianic age. If people from any nation do not journey to Jerusalem to worship the Lord, then the Lord curses those people with a drought. Presumably, the journey to Jerusalem is symbolic while blessings in the messianic age depend on worshiping the Lord.

9

Daniel

The book of Daniel implies that its events and visions took place from 605 BC to 536 BC while Daniel lived in exile and worked in the Babylonian court for both the Neo-Babylonian Empire and the Persian Empire. Also, Daniel 7:1 says that the prophet Daniel wrote down the gist of his vision recorded in Daniel 7. Furthermore, tradition says that the prophet Daniel wrote the book of Daniel in the sixth-century BC. However, many modern day biblical scholars look at the historical and literary evidence in the book of Daniel and conclude that the book was written in the second century BC.[1] Also, some scholars hold to the traditional view of sixth-century authorship while others see evidence of sixth-century origination of some of the literature along with second-century editorship. This debate of sole sixth-century authorship or sixth-century authorship with second-century editorship or sole second-century authorship goes beyond the scope of this book. However, regardless of when the Spirit of God inspired the writing in Daniel, Daniel contributed to end-time prophecy. This chapter focuses on the six apocalypses in Daniel 2, 4, and 7–12.

---

1. See LaSor et al., *Old Testament Survey*, chapter 43.

DANIEL 2

Background from Daniel 1

According to Daniel 1, Babylonian king Nebuchadnezzar in 605 BC exiled many Israelites into Babylon, which included the teenaged Daniel. The king also recruited Daniel and three other highly capable Israelites to train for work in the Babylonian court. Daniel and his three Israelite colleagues/friends excelled in their training that included the study of Babylonian literature and philosophy. And Daniel could understand all kinds of visions and dreams.

The Content of Daniel 2

In Daniel 2:1–6, King Nebuchadnezzar in 604 BC felt troubled by one of his dreams. He summoned his leading wise men including magicians, enchanters, sorcerers, and astrologers. The king told his wise men that his dream troubled him and he wanted to know the meaning of his dream. The wise men asked the king to tell them his dream so they could interpret it for him. But the king refused to tell them his dream and said that he firmly decided that the wise men must tell the king both his dream and the interpretation of his dream or he would cut them into pieces and turn their houses into rubble. If they correctly reported his dream and the interpretation, then he would give them gifts, rewards, and honor.

In Daniel 2:7–9, the wise men again asked the king to tell them his dream so they could interpret it for him. The king told them he suspected that they would tell him lies instead of the real meaning of the dream. The king again asked them to tell him both the dream and its interpretation or they would suffer the penalty of death.

In Daniel 2:10–13, the astrologers told that king that no human could do what the king demanded. They said that nobody but the gods could reveal the dream and the gods do not live among men. This response infuriated the king and he gave orders to execute all of the wise men in Babylon. The king sent his guards to look for and execute Daniel and his three Israelite friends.

In Daniel 2:14–16, the commander of the king's guards found Daniel. Daniel spoke to the commander with wisdom and tact. Then,

Daniel went to the king to ask for time so Daniel could interpret the dream for the king.

In Daniel 2:17-23, Daniel returned to his home and explained the situation to his three friends. He asked his friends to join him while pleading to God for mercy concerning the mystery of the dream so the king would not execute Daniel and his friends. During the night, God revealed the dream and its interpretation to Daniel. Then, Daniel praised God.

In Daniel 2:24, Daniel went to the commander of the guards whom the king appointed to execute Daniel. Daniel told the commander, "Do not execute the wise men in Babylon. Take me to the king, and I will interpret his dream for him."

In Daniel 2:25, the commander immediately took Daniel to the king. The commander told the king, "I have found a man among the exiles from Judah who can tell the king what his dream means."

Daniel 2:26-47:

> [26] The king asked Daniel (also called Belteshazzar), "Are you able to tell me what I saw in my dream and interpret it?"
>
> [27] Daniel replied, "No wise man, enchanter, magician or diviner can explain to the king the mystery he has asked about, [28] but there is a God in heaven who reveals mysteries. He has shown King Nebuchadnezzar what will happen in days to come. Your dream and the visions that passed through your mind as you were lying in bed are these:
>
> [29] "As Your Majesty was lying there, your mind turned to things to come, and the revealer of mysteries showed you what is going to happen. [30] As for me, this mystery has been revealed to me, not because I have greater wisdom than anyone else alive, but so that Your Majesty may know the interpretation and that you may understand what went through your mind.
>
> [31] "Your Majesty looked, and there before you stood a large statue—an enormous, dazzling statue, awesome in appearance. [32] The head of the statue was made of pure gold, its chest and arms of silver, its belly and thighs of bronze, [33] its legs of iron, its feet partly of iron and partly of baked clay. [34] While you were watching, a rock was cut out, but not by human hands. It struck the statue on its feet of iron and clay and smashed them. [35] Then the iron, the clay, the bronze, the silver and the gold were all bro-

ken to pieces and became like chaff on a threshing floor in the summer. The wind swept them away without leaving a trace. But the rock that struck the statue became a huge mountain and filled the whole earth.

36 "This was the dream, and now we will interpret it to the king. 37 Your Majesty, you are the king of kings. The God of heaven has given you dominion and power and might and glory; 38 in your hands he has placed all mankind and the beasts of the field and the birds in the sky. Wherever they live, he has made you ruler over them all. You are that head of gold.

39 "After you, another kingdom will arise, inferior to yours. Next, a third kingdom, one of bronze, will rule over the whole earth. 40 Finally, there will be a fourth kingdom, strong as iron—for iron breaks and smashes everything—and as iron breaks things to pieces, so it will crush and break all the others. 41 Just as you saw that the feet and toes were partly of baked clay and partly of iron, so this will be a divided kingdom; yet it will have some of the strength of iron in it, even as you saw iron mixed with clay. 42 As the toes were partly iron and partly clay, so this kingdom will be partly strong and partly brittle. 43 And just as you saw the iron mixed with baked clay, so the people will be a mixture and will not remain united, any more than iron mixes with clay.

44 "In the time of those kings, the God of heaven will set up a kingdom that will never be destroyed, nor will it be left to another people. It will crush all those kingdoms and bring them to an end, but it will itself endure forever. 45 This is the meaning of the vision of the rock cut out of a mountain, but not by human hands—a rock that broke the iron, the bronze, the clay, the silver and the gold to pieces.

"The great God has shown the king what will take place in the future. The dream is true and its interpretation is trustworthy."

46 Then King Nebuchadnezzar fell prostrate before Daniel and paid him honor and ordered that an offering and incense be presented to him. 47 The king said to Daniel, "Surely your God is the God of gods and the Lord of kings and a revealer of mysteries, for you were able to reveal this mystery." (Daniel 2:26–47)

Finally, in Daniel 2:48–49, the king promoted Daniel to a high position in the Babylonian royal court while lavishing him with gifts. Also, at the request of Daniel, the king appointed Daniel's three friends as administrators over the province of Babylon while Daniel stayed at the royal court.

Discussion of Daniel 2

Ironically, many Christians see Nebuchadnezzar as a prefiguration of the final antichrist/beast in Revelation while Daniel 2 said that Nebuchadnezzar fell prostrate before Daniel. For example, Revelation used the city of Babylon to symbolically describe evil governmental forces that oppose the people of God in the end times. And Nebuchadnezzar's sack and destruction of Jerusalem understandably made him a prefiguration of the beast. However, the Lord deeply loved Nebuchadnezzar while Daniel 2 showed the Lord giving Nebuchadnezzar a dream about the eventual rise and fall of earthly kingdoms and the supernatural emergence of the kingdom of God in the messianic age.

This dream of Nebuchadnezzar and its interpretation fits the description of an apocalypse. For instance, as noted in chapters 1 and 8, an apocalyptic vision or dream includes important events that involve divine intervention while a divinely appointed mediator helps to interpret the vision. In the case of Daniel 2, the king dreamt about major future events in human history such as the eventual emergence of the messianic age and then the prophet Daniel appeared while interpreting the dream.

This apocalypse described the rise and fall of four successive earthly empires followed by the emergence of the kingdom of God. Daniel unequivocally identified the first empire as the Neo-Babylonian Empire. Scholars debate the identity of the next three empires while the following scenario might fit the prophecy. In the first succession, Cyrus overthrew the Neo-Babylonian Empire while his empire is called the Persian Empire or the Achaemenid Empire. In the second succession, Alexander of Macedonia overthrew the Persian Empire and established the brief Hellenistic Empire while four of his generals eventually succeeded him and established Hellenistic kingdoms. In the third succession, Rome conquered all Hellenistic kingdoms and the rest of the Mediterranean. This identification of the empires might oversimplify the prophecy while the exact identity of the three earthly successions has no impact on the prophecy's announcement of the supernatural emergence of the kingdom of God. Also, according to conditional futurism, any of the four respective earthly empires could have turned to the Lord and survived if they continued to serve the Lord. However, any such conversion of an ancient empire would have radically changed the nature of the empire. Perhaps such a conversion came closest with the Roman Empire, but the Roman Empire failed to turn to the Lord in various ways.

DANIEL 4

Content of Daniel 4

Daniel 4 recounts the second apocalyptic dream of Babylonian king Nebuchadnezzar. Chapter 1 already looked at Daniel 4:19–27. Also, the biblical author wrote 4:1–18 and 4:34–37 in the first person of Nebuchadnezzar and 4:19–33 in the third person.

In Daniel 4:1–8, Nebuchadnezzar pronounced a blessing to people in every nation and praised God for his miraculous signs and everlasting kingdom. Then, Nebuchadnezzar said that he felt content in his palace and prosperity, but a dream made him afraid. So he commanded his wise men to come to him interpret his dream. He told them the dream, but nobody could interpret it for him. Finally, Daniel arrived.

In Daniel 4:9–13, Nebuchadnezzar began recounting his dream to Daniel. In the vision of his dream, Nebuchadnezzar saw an enormous tree in the middle of the land. The tree grew large and strong while it reached the top of the sky and people could see it from the ends of the earth. The tree leaves looked beautiful and the abundant fruit fed every creature. The beasts on the ground found shelter under the tree while birds in the air lived in the branches. Then, a messenger from heaven appeared to Nebuchadnezzar.

Daniel 4:14–17:

> [14] He [the messenger from heaven] called in a loud voice: "Cut down the tree and trim off its branches; strip off its leaves and scatter its fruit. Let the animals flee from under it and the birds from its branches. [15] But let the stump and its roots, bound with iron and bronze, remain in the ground, in the grass of the field.
>
> "Let him be drenched with the dew of heaven, and let him live with the animals among the plants of the earth. [16] Let his mind be changed from that of a man and let him be given the mind of an animal, till seven times pass by for him.
>
> [17] "The decision is announced by messengers, the holy ones declare the verdict, so that the living may know that the Most High is sovereign over all kingdoms on earth and gives them to anyone he wishes and sets over them the lowliest of people." (Daniel 4:14–17)

In Daniel 4:18, Nebuchadnezzar asked Daniel to interpret the dream.

In Daniel 4:19, Daniel felt perplexed and terrified. Nebuchadnezzar told Daniel, "Do not let the dream or its meaning alarm you."

In Daniel 4:20–27, Daniel interpreted the dream. The enormous tree represented Nebuchadnezzar. Through the heavenly messenger, God issues a decree that he would drive Nebuchadnezzar away from people and he would live like a wild animal. He would eat grass in the same way cattle eat grass, and dew from the sky would drench him. Seven periods of time would pass and then he would acknowledge that God sovereignly rules over human governments. The command to leave the tree stump meant that God would restore the Babylonian Empire to Nebuchadnezzar when he would acknowledge that God rules. Daniel pleaded with Nebuchadnezzar to repent of his wickedness by doing what is right such as helping the oppressed. Also, the repentance might prevent the prophesied interruption of Nebuchadnezzar's reign as king.

In Daniel 4:28–37, the dream came true after twelve months. Nebuchadnezzar walked on the roof of his palace and boasted to himself about his great power and his great empire. Suddenly a heavenly messenger appeared and pronounced the judgment from 4:14–17. Immediately, Nebuchadnezzar was driven away from people and ate grass in the same way that cattle eat grass. Dew from the sky drenched his body. His hair grew like feathers of an eagle. His nails grew like bird claws. At the end of that time, Nebuchadnezzar raised his eyes toward heaven and he regained his sanity. He praised and glorified God. At the same time, he regained his honor and the splendor of his kingdom. His advisers and nobles sought him. He again sat on his thrown and developed greater political power than before his insanity.

Discussion of Daniel 4

God showed his love to Nebuchadnezzar. As discussed earlier, Nebuchadnezzar's ruthlessness to Jerusalem made him a prefiguration of the final antichrist/ beast in Revelation. Despite this ruthlessness and prophecies from Isaiah and Jeremiah against Babylon, God gave a second apocalyptic dream to Nebuchadnezzar while showing him God's desire to restore Nebuchadnezzar. Likewise, Daniel 4 taught about a repentant and restored prefiguration of the antichrist. And as described in chapter 1, Daniel 4 also taught about the conditional dynamics of apocalyptic judgments.

DANIEL 7

Content of Daniel 7

In Daniel 7:1, during the first year of the co-regency of Babylonian king Belshazzar (around 553 BC), Daniel dreamt visions while lying on his bed and wrote down the gist of his dream.

In Daniel 7:2–7, Daniel dreamt and saw four winds of heaven stir the great sea. Four beasts arose from the sea. The first beast looked like a lion with eagle's wings. Eventually, the wings were torn off, and the beast was lifted up until it stood like a man, and it was given the heart of man. Then, the second beast looked like a bear. It was raised up and held three ribs in its teeth. After that, the third beast looked like a four-headed leopard with four wings like a bird, and it ruled with authority. Lastly, the fourth beast looked terrifying and powerful. It used large iron teeth to crush and devour its victims while trampling underfoot whatever was left. And ten horns protruded from the beast.

In Daniel 7:8, Daniel thought about the ten horns of the beast, and then a little horn arose and uprooted three of the other horns. This horn saw with human-like eyes and spoke boastfully.

In Daniel 7:9–10, Daniel saw thrones appear and the Ancient of Days sat on his throne. His clothing looked white like snow and his hair white like wool. His throne blazed with flames while a river of fire flowed out from him. Ten thousand times ten thousand angels stood before him. The court began its session while books opened.

In Daniel 7:11, the horn of the fourth beast kept boasting. Then, the beast fell dead and was thrown into the blazing fire.

In Daniel 7:12, the other beasts had lost their authority and continued to live for a period of time.

In Daniel 7:13–14, "one like a son of man" approached and entered into the presence of the Ancient of Days. The Ancient of Days gave one like a son of man sovereign power over all nations while people of every language worship him. His sovereignty would last forever.

In Daniel 7:15–18, Daniel felt troubled about his vision and asked an angel to interpret it. The angel said that the four beasts are four kingdoms that will rise from the people of the earth. And the saints of the Most High (God) would eventually posses the kingdom forever.[2]

---

2. *Saints* according to the Bible are ordinary or extraordinary people dedicated to

In Daniel 7:19–22, Daniel wanted to know more about the fourth beast, the most terrifying of the beasts. That beast had ten horns on its head, iron teeth, and bronze claws. It crushed and devoured victims. The final little horn on the head of that beast eventually looked more powerful than the other horns. As Daniel watched, the final horn waged war against the saints of God and defeated them. Then, the Ancient of Days arrived and pronounced judgment in favor of the saints of the Most High while they ended up possessing the kingdom.

In Daniel 7:23–25, the angel explained to Daniel that the fourth beast would be a fourth kingdom that arises on the earth and devours the earth, tramples it, and crushes it. The ten horns are ten kings from the fourth kingdom. Then, another king arises from the fourth kingdom and subdues three of the original kings from the fourth kingdom. This final king speaks against the Lord and oppresses the saints for three and a half periods of time.

In Daniel 7:26–27, the divine court began its session. The final horn loses his power and is taken away forever. Then, the saints of the Most High receive the power and greatness of all earthly kingdoms. The Most High's kingdom becomes an everlasting kingdom, and all earthly rulers worship and obey him.

In Daniel 7:28, the vision ended while Daniel felt troubled and kept the matter to himself.

Discussion of Daniel 7

Assuming the succession of the four kingdoms in Daniel 2, as stated earlier, went from (1) the Neo-Babylonian Empire to (2) the Persian Empire to (3) the Hellenistic (Greek) kingdoms to (4) the Roman Empire, the succession of the four kingdoms in Daniel 7 could be the same. And Daniel 7 put the spotlight on the little horn of the fourth kingdom and the kingdom of God ruled by the Ancient of Days. However, the three and a half periods of time also suggests that the little horn is the Hellenistic king Antiochus IV Epiphanes.[3] Likewise, this apocalypse might focus more on theme instead of chronology while involving multiple fulfillments.

God, which includes all genuine believers in the biblical God. The post-biblical traditional definition of *Saint* means "extraordinary people dedicated to God and officially recognized by the church."

3. See this chapter's sections Daniel 8–12 for more about Antiochus.

The horns in the fourth kingdom represent power and royal rulers. The little horn started small, but grew to become the largest horn.

In the case of the fourth kingdom being the Roman Empire and the little horn being a Roman emperor, then Revelation 17:9–11 drew upon this while referring to the seven heads of the beast as both the capital city of Rome and a series of Roman emperors.[4] Perhaps the eighth king in 17:9–11 coincided with the little horn of the beast. In Daniel 7, the little horn boasted while rising to rule the fourth kingdom and defeating the saints of God for three and a half periods of time.[5] Then, the Ancient of Days arrived and gave the kingdom of God to the saints. The little horn ended up in the blazing fire flowing from the throne of God.

Jesus Christ called himself "the Son of Man" dozens of times in the four Gospels, which referred to Daniel 7:13–14. Also, in Revelation 1:14, the hair of Jesus looked white like wool, comparable to the hair of the Ancient of Days in Daniel 7:9–10. Additionally, Daniel 7:22 said that the arrival of the Ancient of Days would end the reign of the little horn of the beast and begin the kingdom of God. Furthermore, verses 7:14 and 7:27 referred to the divine kingdom respectively as his (the son of man's) kingdom and his (the Most High's) kingdom. These juxtapositions identify the Son of Man with the Most High.

DANIEL 8

Content of Daniel 8

In Daniel 8:1–4, during the third year of the co-regency of Babylonian king Belshazzar (around 551 BC), Daniel saw another vision. He saw himself in the fortress of Susa near the Ulai Canal.[6] Daniel saw a ram with two long horns standing beside the canal. One of the horns grew longer than the other. The ram charged to the west, north and south. No animal could stand against the ram, and he became great.

In Daniel 8:5–8, a goat with a prominent horn between his eyes appeared from the west. The goat charged and raged toward the ram.

---

4. See chapter 1.

5. The three and a half periods of time could be three and a half years or three and a half indefinite periods of time.

6. About twenty years after the third year of the co-regency of Belshazzar (around 530 BC), Persian emperor Cambyses made Susa the capital of the Persian Empire. And in 331 BC, Alexander of Macedonia defeated Susa and the Persian Empire.

The goat furiously struck the ram, shattered the two horns of the ram, knocked the ram to the ground, and trampled him. The goat became great, but his horn broke off in the height of his power. Four prominent horns replaced the broken off large horn, and they grew up toward the four winds of heaven.

In Daniel 8:9–12, a small horn came from the four prominent horns, and he grew in power from the south to the east, including the Beautiful Land (Jerusalem). The horn grew until it reached the heavenly host, and he threw some of the heavenly host down to earth and trampled on them. He made himself as great as the Prince of the host. The horn removed the daily sacrifices from the Prince and lowered the place of the sacrifices. Rebellion caused the host and the daily sacrifice to fall into the control of the horn. The horn prospered in everything he did and threw truth to the ground.

In Daniel 8:13–14, holy angels spoke:

> [13] Then I heard a holy one speaking, and another holy one said to him, "How long will it take for the vision to be fulfilled—the vision concerning the daily sacrifice, the rebellion that causes desolation, the surrender of the sanctuary and the trampling underfoot of the LORD's people?"
>
> [14] He said to me, "It will take 2,300 evenings and mornings; then the sanctuary will be reconsecrated." (Daniel 8:13–14)

In Daniel 8:15–16, Daniel saw somebody that looked like a man. He heard a man's voice calling from the Ulai canal. The voice said, "Gabriel, tell this man the meaning of the vision."

In Daniel 8:17, the angel Gabriel walked toward Daniel. Daniel felt terrified and fell prostrate. "Son of man," Gabriel said to Daniel, "understand that the vision concerns the time of the end."

In Daniel 8:18, Daniel fell into a deap sleep with his face on the ground. Then, Gabriel touched Daniel and raised him to his feet.

In Daniel 8:19–26:

> [19] He said: "I am going to tell you what will happen later in the time of wrath, because the vision concerns the appointed time of the end. [20] The two-horned ram that you saw represents the kings of Media and Persia. [21] The shaggy goat is the king of Greece, and the large horn between its eyes is the first king. [22] The four horns that replaced the one that was broken off represent four

> kingdoms that will emerge from his nation but will not have the same power.
>
> ²³ "In the latter part of their reign, when rebels have become completely wicked, a fierce-looking king, a master of intrigue, will arise. ²⁴ He will become very strong, but not by his own power. He will cause astounding devastation and will succeed in whatever he does. He will destroy those who are mighty, the holy people. ²⁵ He will cause deceit to prosper, and he will consider himself superior. When they feel secure, he will destroy many and take his stand against the Prince of princes. Yet he will be destroyed, but not by human power.
>
> ²⁶ "The vision of the evenings and mornings that has been given you is true, but seal up the vision, for it concerns the distant future." (Daniel 8:19–26)

In Daniel 8:27, Daniel felt exhausted and ill for several days, then he got up and continued with his work in the Babylonian court. And Daniel could not understand the vision.

Discussion of Daniel 8

This apocalyptic prophecy referred to the Persian Empire and the Hellenistic (Greek) kingdoms. Historians commonly refer to "the kings of Media and Persia" as the kings of the Achaemenid Empire or merely the Persian Empire because Persia conquered Media. One of the two long horns of the ram represented Media while the other horn represented Persia. The longer of the two horns represented the dominance of Persia. Also, the goat with a single horn represented Alexander of Macedonia while the four replacement horns represented prominent Hellenistic kingdoms that divided Alexander's empire after the death of Alexander. For example, after the lack of an obvious heir to the throne of Alexander, some of his former generals fought wars with each other and partitioned Alexander's conquests while establishing Hellenistic kingdoms. The four primary Hellenistic kingdoms were the Seleucid Empire founded by Seleucus, the Ptolemaic kingdom founded by Ptolemy, the kingdom founded by Cassander, and the kingdom founded by Lysimachus. Additionally, Seleucus and Ptolemy also founded major dynasties for their kingdoms, respectively the Seleucid dynasty and the Ptolemaic dynasty.

The Persian Empire and the Hellenistic kingdoms respectively granted religious freedom to the Jews (Judahites/Israelites) in Jerusalem for over three centuries until the 175 BC rise of the eighth successor of the Hellenistic Seleucid Empire, King Antiochus IV Epiphanes. Daniel 8 referred to Antiochus as the small horn that would arise from the four Hellenistic kingdoms and grow big.

In 175 BC, Antiochus usurped the Seleucid throne from a relative and opposed the "Prince of princes," which was the anointed Jewish high priest Onias III, the most influential leader among the Jews in Jerusalem. Antiochus opposed Onias III by removing him from the Jewish high priesthood. Also, Antiochus caused desolation by trampling the host (Jews) and removing their daily sacrifice. For instance, around 168 BC, Antiochus notoriously overthrew Jerusalem and slaughtered an estimated forty thousand Jews. Then, he desecrated the Jewish temple by entering it and touching holy objects and offerings. Soon after that, he completely desecrated the Jewish temple by outlawing the biblical sacrifices, making the Jewish temple of the Lord into a temple of Zeus, and sacrificing biblically abominable things in the temple such as swine.[7] Antiochus continued to persecute Jews who followed their biblical laws. This sparked a three-year revolution led by Mattathias and his son Judas Maccabee. Finally, in 165 BC, the Jews overthrew the Seleucid army in Jerusalem. This led to the rededication of the Jewish temple and the annual celebration of Hanukkah, which means "dedication."

That revolution and rededication evidently fulfilled Daniel 8:14: "It will take 2,300 evenings and mornings; then the sanctuary will be reconsecrated." For example, Exodus 29:38–39 taught that Israelite priests performed evening and morning sacrifices everyday. And 2,300 evening and morning sacrifices takes a little more than three years, which approximated the length of time that Antiochus abolished Jewish biblical sacrifices.

Additional background to these events includes that Onias III reigned as the Jewish high priest from 185 BC to 175 BC. He took a strong stand for biblical traditions while traditional Jews and Hellenistic Jews developed tension between themselves, tensions that nearly started

---

7. See a record of atrocities committed by Antiochus in the Apocrypha, book of 2 Maccabees 5–6. Also, Leviticus 11:4–8 listed swine among ceremoniously unclean mammals.

a civil war.[8] In 175 BC, Antiochus removed Onias III from the high priesthood while giving the priesthood to the highest bidder, which was Onias's brother Jason, a Hellenistic Jew. In 170 BC, conspirators murdered Onias III. In 164 BC, Antiochus died of disease. Also, Daniel 9–12 referred to various people and events in Daniel 8.

DANIEL 9

Content of Daniel 9

In Daniel 9:1–19, during the first regnal year of Babylonian king Darius the Mede in 538 BC, Daniel understood from the scriptures of the prophet Jeremiah that the desolation of Jerusalem would last seventy years. Then, Daniel turned to the Lord and pleaded with him in prayer. Daniel appealed to the Lord's greatness and faithfulness to keep his promises to those who love and obey him. Daniel repented of the sins of the Israelites while acknowledging that the Lord brought the disaster on Jerusalem because the Israelites disobeyed the Lord. And Daniel asked the Lord to look with favor upon the "desolation" of his sanctuary.

Daniel 9:20–27 described Daniel's vision that appeared while he continued to pray:

> [20] While I was speaking and praying, confessing my sin and the sin of my people Israel and making my request to the LORD my God for his holy hill— [21] while I was still in prayer, Gabriel, the man I had seen in the earlier vision, came to me in swift flight about the time of the evening sacrifice. [22] He instructed me and said to me, "Daniel, I have now come to give you insight and understanding. [23] As soon as you began to pray, a word went out, which I have come to tell you, for you are highly esteemed. Therefore, consider the word and understand the vision:
>
> [24] "Seventy 'sevens' are decreed for your people and your holy city to finish transgression, to put an end to sin, to atone for wickedness, to bring in everlasting righteousness, to seal up vision and prophecy and to anoint the Most Holy Place.
>
> [25] "Know and understand this: From the time the word goes out to restore and rebuild Jerusalem until the Anointed One, the ruler, comes, there will be seven 'sevens,' and sixty-two 'sevens.' It will be rebuilt with streets and a trench, but in times of trouble.

---

8. Hellenistic Jews incorporated Greek culture with traditional Jewish culture.

²⁶ After the sixty-two 'sevens,' the Anointed One will be put to death and will have nothing. The people of the ruler who will come will destroy the city and the sanctuary. The end will come like a flood: War will continue until the end, and desolations have been decreed. ²⁷ He will confirm a covenant with many for one 'seven.' In the middle of the 'seven' he will put an end to sacrifice and offering. And at the temple he will set up an abomination that causes desolation, until the end that is decreed is poured out on him." (Daniel 9:20–27)

Discussion of Daniel 9

No historical sources beside the book of Daniel identify this Darius the Mede, and Daniel 5:31—6:28 implies that he ruled in Babylon immediately after Cyrus overthrew Babylon. Likewise, the first regnal year of Darius set Daniel 9 in 538 BC. At that time, Daniel read from Jeremiah that the desolation of Jerusalem and its temple would last seventy years. Nebuchadnezzar destroyed Jerusalem and its temple in 586, which was forty-eight years of desolation. However, Nebuchadnezzar in 605 overthrew Egyptian control of Judah and Jerusalem, which resulted in sixty-seven years of Babylonian control while sixty-seven years rounds to seventy years. Evidently, Daniel calculated the seventy years of desolation from the beginning of Babylonian control over Jerusalem. And Daniel interpreted a quick end to the desolation, especially in the light of the fall of Babylon.

The angel Gabriel appeared to Daniel while he earnestly prayed. Gabriel said, "desolations have been decreed," implying a decree from God. While Daniel prayed about restoration from the Babylonian desolation of Jerusalem and its temple, Gabriel announced the end of the Babylonian desolation and the rebuilding of Jerusalem and also announced more desolation in the future. This sobering announcement taught that desolations are a motif in human history. The Babylonian desolation of Jerusalem was a prefiguration of future desolations.

Gabriel also referred to the decree to restore Jerusalem, which first occurred in 605 BC as recorded in Jeremiah 25 when the Lord decreed that the Babylonian exile would last seventy years. This divine decree also foreshadowed four other decrees: (1) the 538 BC decree by Cyrus that Jews should return to Jerusalem and restore its temple,[9] (2) the 520 BC

---

9. See 2 Chronicles 36:22–23 and Ezra 1:1–4.

decree by Persian king Darius that enforced Cyrus's decree for the Jews to return to Jerusalem and restore its temple,[10] (3) the 458 BC decree by Persian king Artaxerxes that Ezra and any volunteer Jew in his kingdom could take wealth from the Persian treasury and go to Jerusalem,[11] and (4) the 444 BC letter from Artaxerxes for his cup bearer, the Israelite Nehemiah, to help rebuild the walls of Jerusalem.[12]

Gabriel said in Daniel 9:24 that "seventy 'sevens'" are decreed for the Jews and Jerusalem "to finish transgression, to put an end to sin, to atone for wickedness, to bring in everlasting righteousness, to seal up vision and prophecy and to anoint the Most Holy Place." The "seventy 'sevens'" referred to a period of time that might have been years. The literal interpretation for "seventy 'sevens'" is seventy times seven that equals 490 years. Regardless of the literalness of these years, Gabriel took the seventy years of the Babylonian desolation and multiplied by seven while the biblical number *seven* is a motif that implies completion.[13] This period of time would end and make amends for sin and begin everlasting righteousness. Also, Daniel 9:25 said that after "the sixty-two 'sevens,' the Anointed One will be put to death." This initially described the 170 BC murder of the former anointed High Priest Onias III.[14] In this case, a literal interpretation of the "the sixty-two 'sevens' was 434 years, which was one year off the exact number of years from the beginning of Babylonian dominance in 605 to the murder of Onias III in 170 BC. And the rest of 9:25 said that the people of the ruler would come to destroy the city and sanctuary, which included the 9:27 *abomination that causes desolation*.

The phrase *abomination that causes desolation* also appears in Daniel 11:31, Daniel 12:11, Matthew 24:15, and Mark 13:14. That phrase paralleled the Daniel 8:13 phrase *rebellion that causes desolation*. The rebellion of Antiochus discussed in the section on Daniel 8 included the abomination. For instance, the abomination specially referred to Antiochus desecrating the Jewish temple by touching holy objects, outlawing the biblical sacrifices, making the Jewish temple of the Lord into a temple of Zeus, and sacrificing biblically abominable things in

10. See Ezra 6:1–12.
11. See Ezra 7:11–26.
12. See Nehemiah 2:1–9.
13. See Bullinger, *Number in Scripture*, 150–151.
14. The previous section on Daniel 8 introduced Onias III.

the temple such as swine. That abomination followed Antiochus and his army's notorious overthrow of Jerusalem and slaughter of an estimated forty thousand Jews.

Jesus Christ in Matthew 24:15 and Mark 13:14 referred to the "abomination that causes desolation" as a future event. Jesus referred to a past event while implying that event foreshadowed a future event. Likewise, Jesus taught and prophesied that the abomination and desolation from Antiochus was a prefiguration of a future event.

After the respective prophecy of Jesus, the next abomination that causes desolation involved the AD 70 destruction of Jerusalem. In this desolation, Roman general Titus and his army surrounded Jerusalem, slaughtered hundreds of thousands of Jews, heaped and burned many dead Jews around the Jewish altar, and destroyed the entire Jewish temple by fire except the retaining walls.[15] And as stated above, Gabriel prophesied that the Babylonian desolation was a prefiguration of the Antiochus desolation, which established a biblical motif of desolation. Also, another prefiguration in Daniel 9 was the murder of the "Anointed One" Onias III foreshadowing the death of Christ.

DANIEL 10-12

Highlights of Daniel 10-12

Daniel 10-12 is the longest and final apocalypse in Daniel. It developed details from the events in Daniel 8-9 and climaxed with a resurrection of both the righteous and the wicked.

In Daniel 10:1-2, during the third regnal year of Cyrus in 537 BC, Daniel received a divine revelation concerning a great war. Daniel humbled himself before God by mourning for three weeks while abstaining from luxuries such as choice food, wine, and skin lotion. Then, Daniel saw a vision that explained to him the original revelation.

In Daniel 10:3—11:1, Daniel stood on the bank of the Tigris River in Mesopotamia and looked up. He saw a man dressed in linen with a gold belt, a face like lightening, eyes like flaming torches, arms and legs with a bright bronze glow, and a voice that sounded like a multitude of people. The sight made Daniel lose his strength. Then, he heard the man speak, and Daniel fell into a deep sleep. The man touched Daniel and

---

15. Josephus, *The Wars of the Jews,* book 6, chapter 4.

stood him on his feet. The man said that God heard Daniel's prayers from the first day that he prayed and humbled himself before God. The man said that he came in response to Daniel's prayers. But the prince of the Persian kingdom resisted the man for twenty-one days until "Michael, one of the chief princes," came to help the man deliver this message to Daniel. Daniel lost his strength and fell to the ground two more times, and each time the man strengthened and stood Daniel on his feet. The man said that he would soon return to fight against the prince of Persia, and then the prince of Greece would arrive. And nobody supported the man except "Michael, your prince."

Daniel 11:2–4 described the succession of Persian kings and the rise of a great Greek ruler. The kingdom of the Greek ruler would weaken and parcel out to the four winds.

In Daniel 11:5–20, two kings would succeed the great Greek ruler, divide his kingdom, and establish major dynasties: the dynasty of the South and the dynasty of the North. These two dynasties would develop a history of covenants and wars with each other.

In Daniel 11:21–35, a contemptible person without royal title would seize the dynastic throne of the North. He would fight various battles and both make and break a covenant. His armed forces would "desecrate the temple fortress," "abolish the daily sacrifice," and "set up the abomination that causes desolation."

In Daniel 11:35–45, this king would exalt himself above every god and against the God of gods while he disregards the gods of his fathers. He would honor a god of military fortress and attack the mightiest fortresses with the help of a foreign god. The king of the South would battle against the self-exalted king, but he storms against the king of the South and gains all the treasures of Egypt and the neighboring lands. The self-exalted king would hear alarming reports from the east and north, which sets him into a great rage while he starts to destroy many people. He pitches his tent in the beautiful holy mountain. "Yet he will come to his end, and no one will help him."

In Daniel 12:1–13:

> [1] "At that time Michael, the great prince who protects your people, will arise. There will be a time of distress such as has not happened from the beginning of nations until then. But at that time your people—everyone whose name is found written in the book—will be delivered. [2] Multitudes who sleep in the dust of the earth will awake: some to everlasting life, others to shame and

everlasting contempt. ³ Those who are wise will shine like the brightness of the heavens, and those who lead many to righteousness, like the stars for ever and ever. ⁴ But you, Daniel, roll up and seal the words of the scroll until the time of the end. Many will go here and there to increase knowledge."

⁵ Then I, Daniel, looked, and there before me stood two others, one on this bank of the river and one on the opposite bank. ⁶ One of them said to the man clothed in linen, who was above the waters of the river, "How long will it be before these astonishing things are fulfilled?"

⁷ The man clothed in linen, who was above the waters of the river, lifted his right hand and his left hand toward heaven, and I heard him swear by him who lives forever, saying, "It will be for a time, times and half a time. When the power of the holy people has been finally broken, all these things will be completed."

⁸ I heard, but I did not understand. So I asked, "My lord, what will the outcome of all this be?"

⁹ He replied, "Go your way, Daniel, because the words are rolled up and sealed until the time of the end. ¹⁰ Many will be purified, made spotless and refined, but the wicked will continue to be wicked. None of the wicked will understand, but those who are wise will understand.

¹¹ "From the time that the daily sacrifice is abolished and the abomination that causes desolation is set up, there will be 1,290 days. ¹² Blessed is the one who waits for and reaches the end of the 1,335 days.

¹³ "As for you, go your way till the end. You will rest, and then at the end of the days you will rise to receive your allotted inheritance." (Daniel 12:1–13)

Discussion of Daniel 10–12

Daniel sees a revelation about a great war. He responded with mourning, prayer, and fasting for three weeks from luxuries such as choice food, wine, and skin lotion. Then, a heavenly man, an angel, appears and interprets the initial revelation.

Daniel 10:3—11:1 in part teaches about angels of God's people and their enemy forces of evil in the heavenly realms. For example, Daniel saw an unnamed heavenly angel referred to as a "man" who acted as both a messenger to humans and a warrior against "the prince of the Persia" and "the prince of Greece." The prince of Persia resisted this angel for twenty-one days, clearly implying a spiritual event or at least spiritual imagery. Additionally, Daniel 10–12 refers to Michael as "one of the chief princes," "your prince," and "the great prince who protects your people" while Jude 12 identified Michael as an archangel. The title *prince* implies a high rank while *prince* might relate to Ephesians 6:12 teaching about fighting "against the rulers, against the authorities, against the powers of this dark world and against the spiritual forces of evil in the heavenly realms." Also, this vision helped Daniel to understand the original divine revelation about a great war. Likewise, the first battles recorded in this apocalypse are the battles of the unnamed angel and Michael versus the princes of Persia and Greece.

Daniel 11:5–20 discusses various wars and covenants between the Hellenistic Ptolemaic dynasty and the Hellenistic Seleucid dynasty.[16] For instance, "the king of the South" and his successors refers to the Ptolemaic dynasty who ruled Egypt, south of Jerusalem. And "the king of the North" and his successors refers to the Seleucid dynasty who ruled from Syria and Babylonia, north of Jerusalem. The Ptolemaic kings originally ruled Jerusalem, but the Seleucid Empire battled against the Ptolemaic kingdom and eventually took control of Jerusalem. This set the stage for Antiochus, the eighth successor of the Seleucid dynasty and the archenemy in Daniel 8–9.

Daniel 11:21–35 clearly describes events in the life of Antiochus. His armed forces desecrate the temple fortress, abolish the daily sacrifice, and set up the abomination that causes desolation.

The narrative flow of Daniel 11:36–45 appears to describe the same king as in verses 11:21–35. But verses 11:36–45 describes events not in the reign of Antiochus while verses 11:21–35 describes events during the reign of Antiochus. Also, Daniel 11:2–35 nearly literally describes events in Persian and Hellenistic history while 11:36–45 departed from known history, except for Antiochus's self-exaltation and death.[17] For example, Daniel 11:37 says that the self-exalted king disregarded the gods of his fathers while Antiochus always honored Zeus, the god of his fathers. And verses 10:40–43 say that the king defeated many coun-

---

16. See the discussion in the section on Daniel 8.

17. Antiochus exalted himself with the title *Epiphanes,* which means "God manifested," while no other Hellenistic king assumed that title.

tries and took the treasures of Egypt while Antiochus failed to take the treasures of Egypt. Three possible interpretations explain this change in the apocalyptic narration. First, Daniel 11:36–45 changed the course of a nearly literal account to a symbolic or hyperbolic account. Second, Daniel 11:36–45 seamlessly started to describe a future king and future events. Third, Daniel 11:36–45 prophesied about Antiochus while the events failed to unfold. The first and second interpretations could fit into apocalyptic symbolism. And the third interpretation would require a reason within the context of biblical conditions. Also, the first and second interpretations could work together. For instance, anything about Antiochus that was literal or symbolic could also represent a prefiguration of future events.

Daniel 12:1–4 climaxes the apocalypse with the arising of the great prince Michael, the greatest distress in history, and the resurrection of multitudes of both righteous people and wicked people. Apocalyptic interpretation need not jump to a literal interpretation of these events. However, in the case of the resurrection, hindsight from the New Testament informs Christian interpreters. Also, the narrative of verse 12:1 said that these events took place "at that time" while the previous verse announced the death of the self-exalted king. In this case, New Testament hindsight informs Christian interpreters of a long delay in the time frame for the resurrection and perhaps also the life and death of another self-exalted king, which fits into the symbolic possibilities of apocalyptic narration.

Daniel 12:5–13 describes Daniel seeing two more angels while he finishes the conversation with the first angel dressed in linen. One of the newly arrived angels asked about the timing of the previously described events. In verse 12:7, the first angel said that it would be for "a time, times and a half time," which many interpret to mean *one time* plus *two times* plus *a half time* that equals three and a half years. And *a time, times and a half time* was the same phrase in Daniel 7:25 that described the length of time that the end-time king would persecute the people of God. Also, verses 12:11–12 refer again to the abolishment of the daily sacrifice and the "abomination that causes desolation." And the 1,290 days in verse 12:11 roughly equaled the three and a half years from verse 12:7 and the duration of the persecution at the hands of Antiochus.[18]

18. The meaning of the Daniel 12:12 blessing of people who persevere 1,335 days, an extension to the standard persecution of three and a half years, remains mysterious.

And in the final verse, 12:13, the angel dressed in linen promised Daniel rest after his sixth-century-BC death until the end when Daniel would arise and receive his reward.

SUMMARY OF END TIMES IN DANIEL

The book of Daniel included six apocalypses. An important theme in Daniel taught about the certain end of ungodly kings who persecute God's people. Daniel 2 prophesied the successive rise and fall of earthly kingdoms followed by the everlasting rise of the kingdom of God. Daniel 4 taught about conditions in apocalyptic judgments and a repentant prefiguration of the antichrist. Daniel 7 paralleled Daniel 2 with the successive rise and fall of earthly kingdoms followed by the everlasting rise of the kingdom of God. And Daniel 7 included the rise and fall of presumably the final king, the antichrist. The three apocalypses in Daniel 8–12 focused on the rise and fall of Antiochus. He presumably was a prefiguration of the end-time antichrist in Daniel 7. Also, the life and death of the anointed High Priest Onias III was a prefiguration of the life and death of Jesus Christ. Additionally, Daniel 12 prophesied the end-time events of the greatest distress and the resurrection.

10

The Gospels

THE PRESENT AND FUTURE KINGDOM OF GOD

In 63 BC, the Jews lost their independence to Rome. During the next ninety years, many Jews developed great expectations for their Messiah to arrive and overthrow Roman rule.

During the late AD 20s, Jesus Christ began preaching to the Jews in Galilee:[1]

> "The time has come," he [Jesus] said. "The kingdom of God has come near. Repent and believe the good news!" (Mark **1:15**)

Jesus taught more about the kingdom of God than anything else. The above verse focuses on both the *conditions* and the *nearness* of the kingdom.

The conditions of the kingdom involve the command to repent and believe. *Repent* means to "change an attitude or view." *Repent* also implies turning from one direction to another. In this case, the change included: (1) turning from disobedience to the Lord and (2) turning from unbelief in the Lord. Also, Jesus upped the requirements of belief by proclaiming that the fulfillment of Old Testament prophecy about the kingdom of God in the messianic age was "near."

During that time, many Jews expected that the Davidic Messiah of Old Testament prophecy would arrive and suddenly overthrow the Roman Empire while establishing the kingdom of God. Jesus understood these expectations and preached that the kingdom was near. However,

---

1. Roman Galilee sat in the land of the former Israelite monarchy and modern day Israel.

the prophetic term *near* refers to time relative to the Lord. Other examples of the prophetic use of *near* include 1 Peter 4:7:

> The end of all things is near. (1 Peter 4:7)

The phrase *The end of all things* in this verse refers to the return of the Lord Jesus Christ bringing human history to completion while fully establishing the kingdom and messianic age. Also, this verse taught about a "near" end of all things. In modern day hindsight, nearly two thousand years have passed without this end.

The paradox of *near* and *two thousand years* sounds hard to reconcile. But 2 Peter 3:3–13 helps to understand this paradox. Verses 3:3–13 teach about the Lord's return while describing scoffers who say, "Where is this 'coming' he promised"? And verses 3:8–9 sheds light on this question by describing time relative to the Lord:

> [8] But do not forget this one thing, dear friends: With the Lord a day is like a thousand years, and a thousand years are like a day. [9] The Lord is not slow in keeping his promise, as some understand slowness. Instead he is patient with you, not wanting anyone to perish, but everyone to come to repentance. (2 Peter 3:8–9)

These verses teach that a thousand years on earth could be like a mere day to the Lord.[2] Likewise, in modern day hindsight, the church has waited nearly two thousand years for the Lord's return while the Lord may see these two thousand years as two days. This helps to understand that the prophetic use of *near* might mean "thousands of years."

In the case of Mark 1:15 at the beginning of this chapter, Jesus preached that the kingdom of God was near while implying both an immediate fulfillment and a long-term fulfillment. Various parables of Jesus such as Matthew 13:24–30 teach about these two fulfillments:

> [24] Jesus told them another parable: "The kingdom of heaven is like a man who sowed good seed in his field. [25] But while everyone was sleeping, his enemy came and sowed weeds among the wheat, and went away. [26] When the wheat sprouted and formed heads, then the weeds also appeared.
>
> [27] The owner's servants came to him and said, 'Sir, didn't you sow good seed in your field? Where then did the weeds come from?'

---

2. Psalm 94:4 also says that one thousand years in God's sight is like a single day.

> ²⁸ "'An enemy did this,' he replied.
>
> "The servants asked him, 'Do you want us to go and pull them up?'
>
> ²⁹ "'No,' he answered, 'because while you are pulling the weeds, you may uproot the wheat with them. ³⁰ Let both grow together until the harvest. At that time I will tell the harvesters: First collect the weeds and tie them in bundles to be burned; then gather the wheat and bring it into my barn.'" (Matthew 13:24–30)

Later that day, Jesus in Matthew 13:37–43 interpreted the parable to his disciples:

> ³⁷ He answered, "The one who sowed the good seed is the Son of Man. ³⁸ The field is the world, and the good seed stands for the people of the kingdom. The weeds are the people of the evil one, ³⁹ and the enemy who sows them is the devil. The harvest is the end of the age, and the harvesters are angels.
>
> ⁴⁰ "As the weeds are pulled up and burned in the fire, so it will be at the end of the age. ⁴¹ The Son of Man will send out his angels, and they will weed out of his kingdom everything that causes sin and all who do evil. ⁴² They will throw them into the blazing furnace, where there will be weeping and gnashing of teeth. ⁴³ Then the righteous will shine like the sun in the kingdom of their Father. Whoever has ears, let them hear." (Matthew 13:37–43)

This parable teaches about two major phases in the kingdom of God. Also, Jesus refers to himself as "the Son of Man," which pointed to the Daniel 7:13–14 messianic "son of man."

The parable teaches about the first phase of the kingdom when the Son of Man and the devil sow seed. This phase begins with Jesus preaching the word of God. And the devil sows bad seed, which represents messages and attitudes that oppose the preaching of Jesus. People who accept the preaching of Jesus gradually grow figuratively into a good crop while people who accept the messages of the devil grow into weeds. Likewise, the first phase of the kingdom includes a world mixed with good and evil.

The second phase of the kingdom includes the harvest that weeds out the evil people and sends them to a fiery judgment while the righteous people shine like the sun. This harvest evidently relates to the Lord's return and results in the kingdom of God with no evil in the world. Also, the righteous shining like the sun describes the righteous after the resurrection. For example, Daniel 12:2–3 says that the righteous at the resurrection "will shine like the brightness of the heavens." Additionally, Jesus teaches that the righteous at the resurrection will resemble angels and no longer die.[3]

JEWISH BACKGROUND TO THE IMAGERY OF JUDGMENT IN THE GOSPELS

Imagery of Judgment in 1 Enoch

Around the third to first century BC, Jewish pseudonymous authors wrote the apocalyptic 1 Enoch.[4] This apocalypse eventually influenced the imagery of judgment in the Gospels and the rest of the New Testament, while this apocalypse also helped to build up Jewish expectations for the sudden appearance of the Messiah and messianic age. The imagery of judgment in 1 Enoch includes fallen angels, unforgivable sin, interim punishment, judgment day, everlasting punishment, darkness, prison, chains, fire, and the abyss. Example passages of 1 Enoch that influenced the language of New Testament judgment include 1 Enoch 10:4–6, 10:11–14, 14:1–7, 17:9–16, 22:2, and 54.

In 1 Enoch 10:4–6, the Lord told the holy angel Raphael to punish the fallen angel Aseal. This passage pictures interim punishment in darkness and judgment day with fire:

> (⁴) To Raphael he [the Lord] said,
> Go, Raphael, and bind Aseal hand and foot, and cast him into the darkness;
> And make an opening in the wilderness that is in Doudael.
> (⁵) Throw him there, and lay beneath him sharp and jagged stones.
> And cover him with darkness, and let him dwell there for an exceedingly long time.
> (⁶) Cover up his face, and let him not see the light.
> And on the day of the great judgment, he will be led away to the burning conflagration.
> (1 Enoch 10:4–6)[5]

---

3. See Matthew 22:23–33, Mark 12:18–27, and Luke 20:27–40.
4. See Nickelsburg and VanderKam, *1 Enoch*, 11.
5. Nickelsburg and VanderKam, 75.

In 1 Enoch 10:11–14, the Lord told the holy angel Michael to punish the fallen angel Shemihazah and all other fallen angels. After they see the death of their children, the fallen angels will be bound for seventy generations until judgment day. Then, they will suffer torture in the prison of the fiery abyss forever. Also, all of the condemned will be bound with them until judgment day, and then sent to judgment:

> (¹¹) And to Michael he said,
> "Go, Michael, bind Shemihazah and the others with him, who have mated with the daughters of men, so that they were defiled by them in their uncleanness.
> (¹²) And when their sons perish and they see the destruction of their beloved ones, bind them for seventy generations in the valleys of the earth, until the day of their judgment is consummated.
> (¹³) Then they will be led away to the fiery abyss, and to the torture, and to the prison where they will be confined forever.
> (¹⁴) And everyone who is condemned and destroyed henceforth will be bound together with them until the consummation of their generation. <And at that time of the judgment, which I shall judge, they will perish for all generations.> (1 Enoch 10:11–14)[6,7]

In 1 Enoch 14:1–7, Enoch tells the fallen angels that the Lord rejects their request for forgiveness for both their sons and themselves.

In 1 Enoch 17:9–16, various rebellious stars and heavenly host at the edge of heaven suffer interim punishment in fire until judgment day.

In 1 Enoch 22:2, the holy angel Uriel oversees "Tartarus," a prison for fallen angels.

In 1 Enoch 54, Enoch sees iron chains of immeasurable weight prepared for the bondage of fallen angels.

---

6. Nickelsburg and VanderKam, 77.

7. The authors of *1 Enoch: A New Translation* translated the Aramaic noun *alam* and its Greek equivalent *aion* to "for an exceedingly long time" in 1 Enoch 10:5 and "forever" in 10:13 because the context of 10:5 was interim punishment while the context of 10:13 was punishment after judgment day. Also, depending on the context, they translated *alam/aion* to "ages," "eternity," "all the ages," "all the days of eternity," "all the generations of eternity," or "from of old." They also translated the adjective to "everlasting" in the context of extended time and to "eternal" in reference to God. (Nickelsburg and VanderKam, 379).

Imagery of Judgment in the Schools of Hillel and Shammai

The schools of Hillel and Shammai were the two most prominent rabbinic schools in the first century AD.[8] The Babylonian Talmud, tract Rosh Hashana, includes tradition about divine judgment from the schools of Hillel and Shammai while the gist of these views likely circulated among the Jews during the life of Jesus:

> The school of Shammai said: There are three divisions of mankind at the Resurrection: the wholly righteous, the utterly wicked, and the average class. The wholly righteous are at once inscribed, and life is decreed for them; the utterly wicked are at once inscribed, and destined for Gehenna, as we read [Dan. xii. 2]: "And many of them that sleep in the dust shall awake, some to everlasting life, and some to shame and everlasting contempt." The third class, the men between the former two, descend to Gehenna, but they weep and come up again, in accordance with the passage [Zech. xiii. 9]: "And I will bring the third part through the fire, and I will refine them as silver is refined, and will try them as gold is tried; and he shall call on My name, and I will answer him." Concerning this last class of men Hannah says [I Sam. ii. 6]: "The Lord causeth to die and maketh alive, He bringeth down to the grave and bringeth up again." The school of Hillel says: The Merciful One inclines (the scale of justice) to the side of mercy, and of this third class of men David says [Psalms, cxvi. 1]: "It is lovely to me that the Lord heareth my voice"; in fact, David applies to them the Psalm mentioned down to the words, "Thou hast delivered my soul from death" [ibid. 8].
>
> Transgressors of Jewish birth and also of non-Jewish birth, who sin with their body descend to Gehenna, and are judged there for twelve months; after that time their bodies are destroyed and burnt, and the winds scatter their ashes under the soles of the feet of the righteous, as we read [Mal. iii. 23]: "And ye shall tread down the wicked, for they shall be as ashes under the soles of your feet"; but as for Minim, informers and disbelievers, who deny the Torah, or Resurrection, or separate themselves from the congregation, or who inspire their fellowmen with dread of them, or who sin and cause others to sin, as did Jeroboam the son of Nebat and his followers, they all descend to Gehenna, and are judged

---

8. Rabbi Hillel (traditionally 110 BC–AD 10) founded the school of Hillel in the late first century BC, which was known for its moderation. Rabbi Shammai (50 BC–AD 30) founded the school of Shammai in the early first century AD, which was known for its strictness.

there from generation to generation, as it is said [Isa. lxvi. ²⁴]: "And they shall go forth and look upon the carcases of the men who have transgressed against Me; for their worm shall not die, neither shall their fire be quenched." Even when Gehenna will be destroyed, they will not be consumed, as it is written [Psalms, xlix. ¹⁵]: "And their forms wasteth away in the nether world," which the sages comment upon to mean that their forms shall endure even when the grave is no more. Concerning them Hannah says [I Sam. ii. ¹⁰]: "The adversaries of the Lord shall be broken to pieces." R. Itz'hac b. Abhin says: "Their faces are black like the sides of a caldron"; while Rabha remarked: "Those who are now the handsomest of the people of Me'huzza will yet be called the children of Gehenna."[9]

This two-paragraph excerpt from tract Rosh Hashana teaches about the fate of the dead. The possible fates of the dead include (1) everlasting life, (2) everlasting punishment in Gehenna, (3) interim punishment in Gehenna and eventual end from annihilation, and (4) interim punishment in Gehenna followed by everlasting life.

The first paragraph of the above excerpt begins by explaining the interpretation of the school of Shammai. Shammai taught about the fate of humanity at the resurrection described in Daniel 12:2. Shammai divided humanity into three classes: (1) the wholly righteous, (2) the utterly wicked, and (3) the average class. As discussed in chapter 9, Daniel 12:2 proclaimed that some would resurrect to "everlasting life" and others to "shame and everlasting contempt." Shammai said that the wholly righteous would resurrect to everlasting life and the utterly wicked would resurrect to shame and everlasting contempt in Gehenna. Also, the average class would resurrect and descend to Gehenna while weeping but then arise to everlasting life. Paradoxically, some people in Gehenna would suffer forever while others in Gehenna would weep and find liberation. Gehenna could cause endless punishment or purgation.

The school of Hillel taught a different view of the average class. Hillel said that the mercy of the Lord inclines to the average class, implying that they never descend to Gehenna.

The second paragraph of the above excerpt describes two possible fates of the wicked dead. First, those who transgress with their bodies would descend to Gehenna for twelve months of punishment and then

9. *The Babylonian Talmud*, Book 2, tract Rosh Hashana, chapter 1.

end from annihilation. Second, the worst transgressors will suffer forever in Gehenna.

SELECTIONS FROM LUKE ON JUDGMENT

Luke 3:1–18

In Luke 3:1–6, during the late AD 20s, John began "preaching a baptism of repentance for the forgiveness of sins."[10]

In Luke 3:7–9:

> [7] John said to the crowds coming out to be baptized by him, "You brood of vipers! Who warned you to flee from the coming wrath? [8] Produce fruit in keeping with repentance. And do not begin to say to yourselves, 'We have Abraham as our father.' For I tell you that out of these stones God can raise up children for Abraham. [9] The ax is already at the root of the trees, and every tree that does not produce good fruit will be cut down and thrown into the fire." (Luke 3:7–9)

In Luke 3:10–14, the crowd including tax collectors and soldiers asked John, "What should we do then?" John said that those with two shirts must share with those who have none; tax collectors must not collect any more taxes than required; and soldiers must not extort money and accuse people falsely.

In Luke 3:15–18:

> [15] The people were waiting expectantly and were all wondering in their hearts if John might possibly be the Messiah. [16] John answered them all, "I baptize you with water. But one who is more powerful than I will come, the straps of whose sandals I am not worthy to untie. He will baptize you with the Holy Spirit and fire. [17] His winnowing fork is in his hand to clear his threshing floor and to gather the wheat into his barn, but he will burn up the chaff with unquenchable fire." [18] And with many other words John exhorted the people and proclaimed the good news to them. (Luke 3:15–18)

John in Luke 3:1–14 taught about water baptism and repentance for the forgiveness of sins. He explained: repentance saves from divine

---

10. *Baptism* means "immersion." John (John the Baptist) performed a religious ceremony called *water baptism*, which involved briefly immersing a person in a body of water.

wrath; repentance must produce the fruit of avoiding evil and doing good deeds; descendants of Abraham (Jews) with no good fruit should expect divine wrath; God can raise up other children for Abraham. John's imagery of judgment shows an ax ready to cut down unproductive trees at their roots before the trees are thrown into fire and end from annihilation.

John in Luke 3:15–18 taught about the coming Messiah and his baptism with the Holy Spirit and fire. The Messiah would immerse (baptize) believers with the Spirit of God and a figurative cleansing fire. John portrays believers as wheat on the Messiah's threshing floor while the Messiah uses his winnowing fork to separate the wheat grain from its chaff (husk). The chaff gets thrown into "unquenchable fire." Likewise, the Messiah and Holy Spirit would purge believers.

Selections from Luke 4–14

Luke 4:33–35:

> 33 In the synagogue there was a man possessed by a demon, an impure spirit. He cried out at the top of his voice, 34 "Go away! What do you want with us, Jesus of Nazareth? Have you come to destroy us? I know who you are—the Holy One of God!"
>
> 35 "Be quiet!" Jesus said sternly. "Come out of him!" Then the demon threw the man down before them all and came out without injuring him. (Luke 4:33–35)

In Luke 4:33–35, a demon possessed a man while the demon asked if he faced destruction from Jesus. Jesus never directly answered the demon's question, but commanded the demon to quiet and come out of the man. Then, the demon left the man according to the command of Jesus.

In Luke 6:37–38, Jesus taught that people are judged, condemned, and forgiven according to the proportion that they judge, condemn, and forgive others.

In Luke 6:49, Jesus said that those who hear his words and never practices them are like a man who builds a house on ground without a foundation. The torrent struck and completely destroyed the house.

In Luke 8:26–37, a demon-possessed man said to Jesus, "I beg you, don't torture me." The demons in the man repetitively begged Jesus "not to order them to go into the Abyss."

In Luke 9:26, Jesus said if people are ashamed of him and his words, then he will be ashamed of them when he returns with his Father's glory and the angels.

In Luke 9:41, Jesus called his generation "unbelieving and perverse" while questioning how long he would stay with them and put up with them.

Luke 10:8–15:

> ⁸ [Jesus said,] "When you enter a town and are welcomed, eat what is offered to you. ⁹ Heal the sick who are there and tell them, 'The kingdom of God has come near to you.' ¹⁰ But when you enter a town and are not welcomed, go into its streets and say, ¹¹ 'Even the dust of your town we wipe from our feet as a warning to you. Yet be sure of this: The kingdom of God has come near.' ¹² I tell you, it will be more bearable on that day for Sodom than for that town.
>
> ¹³ "Woe to you, Chorazin! Woe to you, Bethsaida! For if the miracles that were performed in you had been performed in Tyre and Sidon, they would have repented long ago, sitting in sackcloth and ashes. ¹⁴ But it will be more bearable for Tyre and Sidon at the judgment than for you. ¹⁵ And you, Capernaum, will you be lifted to the heavens? No, you will go down to Hades." (Luke 10:8–15)

In Luke 10:8–12, Jesus said towns that rejected the ministry of the disciples would suffer more than the city of Sodom on judgment day. Jesus referred to the account of the Lord judging and punishing Sodom by destroying it with burning sulfur falling from the sky.[11] Also, in Luke 10:13–15, Jesus warned that the nearby cities of Chorazin, Bethsaida, and Capernaum would suffer greatly on judgment day because they saw great miracles from the disciples and never repented. The judgment of these cites would be worse than the judgment pronounced by Jeremiah on Tyre and Sidon.[12] These judgments imply that the severity of judgment is proportional to the amount of divine revelation that has been rejected.

In Luke 10:17–18, the disciples reported to Jesus that demons submitted to them in Jesus name. Then, Jesus appraised the impact of

---

11. See Genesis 18:16—19:29.
12. See chapter 6.

the disciples' ministry by saying, "I saw Satan fall like lightning from heaven."[13]

In Luke 11:20, Jesus said, "If I drive out demons by the finger of God, then the kingdom of God has come upon you." In this verse, Jesus taught about his judgment of demons and the inauguration of the kingdom of God.

In Luke 11:45-54, Jesus warned Jewish leaders in Jerusalem that they would face judgment for not only their own persecution of Jesus but also for how their ancestors persecuted earlier prophets. This is a case of an accumulative judgment.

In Luke 12:5, Jesus taught to fear God who can throw the dead into hell (Gehenna).

In Luke 12:9, Jesus said that whoever publicly disowns him would be disowned before the angels of God.

In Luke 12:10, Jesus said, "Everyone who speaks a word against the Son of Man will be forgiven, but anyone who blasphemes against the Holy Spirit will not be forgiven." Jesus referred to unpardonable sin. However, Luke in Acts 7:1—8:1 shows Stephen asking God to forgive those who murdered Stephen and blasphemed the Holy Spirit.

In Luke 12:13-21, Jesus warns about judgment of death for those who store wealth for themselves without being rich toward God.

In Luke 12:24-46, Jesus told a parable where the master of a wicked servant will arrive at an unexpected time and "cut him to pieces and assign him a place with the unbelievers."

In Luke 12:47-48, Jesus teaches that people deserve more punishment for intentional disobedience in comparison to ignorant disobedience:

> [47] "The servant who knows the master's will and does not get ready or does not do what the master wants will be beaten with many blows. [48] But the one who does not know and does things deserving punishment will be beaten with few blows. From everyone who has been given much, much will be demanded; and from the one who has been entrusted with much, much more will be asked." (Luke 12:47-48)

In Luke 12:58-59, Jesus taught that civil magistrates mercilessly punish debtors in proportion to their debt:

---

13. See also Ephesians 6:12 and Revelation 12:7-9.

> ⁵⁸ As you are going with your adversary to the magistrate, try hard to be reconciled on the way, or your adversary may drag you off to the judge, and the judge turn you over to the officer, and the officer throw you into prison. ⁵⁹ I tell you, you will not get out until you have paid the last penny." (Luke 12:58–59)

In Luke 13:5, Jesus said to repent or perish, while repentance is a condition for getting saved from perishing.

In Luke 13:6–9, Jesus taught in a parable where the owner of a cultivated tree that produced no fruit for three years gives the tree one more year to start bearing fruit or the owner will stop wasting the soil and cut down the tree.

Luke 13:22–30:

> ²² Then Jesus went through the towns and villages, teaching as he made his way to Jerusalem. ²³ Someone asked him, "Lord, are only a few people going to be saved?"
>
> He said to them, ²⁴ "Make every effort to enter through the narrow door, because many, I tell you, will try to enter and will not be able to. ²⁵ Once the owner of the house gets up and closes the door, you will stand outside knocking and pleading, 'Sir, open the door for us.'
>
> "But he will answer, 'I don't know you or where you come from.'
>
> ²⁶ "Then you will say, 'We ate and drank with you, and you taught in our streets.'
>
> ²⁷ "But he will reply, 'I don't know you or where you come from. Away from me, all you evildoers!'
>
> ²⁸ "There will be weeping there, and gnashing of teeth, when you see Abraham, Isaac and Jacob and all the prophets in the kingdom of God, but you yourselves thrown out. ²⁹ People will come from east and west and north and south, and will take their places at the feast in the kingdom of God. ³⁰ Indeed there are those who are last who will be first, and first who will be last." (Luke 13:22–30)

In Luke 13:22–30, Jesus urged his audience to "enter through the narrow door" and eventually enjoy "the feast of the kingdom of God" at the end of the age. Jesus also cautioned that "many" Jews of his generation would not enter through the narrow door but suffer banishment that includes "weeping" and angry "gnashing of teeth." However, many others from the all around the world will enjoy the feast of the kingdom. The judgment will include surprising twists of the first being last and the last being first.

In Luke 14:16-24, Jesus told a parable about the end-time feast. In the parable, a man prepared a great banquet and invited many guests. When the banquet was ready, the invited guest made excuses for missing the banquet such as somebody needing to take care of a newly purchased field. Then, the man was angry at the excuses and sent his servant to the streets and alleys to invite the poor and disabled. After the servant did this, he told his employer that there was still more room in the banquet. Next, the man sent his servant to the roads and country lanes to compel people to come to the banquet. The man said, "I tell you, not one of those who were invited will get a taste of my banquet." This teaches that the original people invited to the banquet never enjoyed it.

Selections from Luke 16-20

Jesus rebuked Jewish leaders who loved money in both Luke 16:13-15 and 16:19-31—for example:

> [19] [Jesus said,] "There was a rich man who was dressed in purple and fine linen and lived in luxury every day. [20] At his gate was laid a beggar named Lazarus, covered with sores [21] and longing to eat what fell from the rich man's table. Even the dogs came and licked his sores.
>
> [22] "The time came when the beggar died and the angels carried him to Abraham's side. The rich man also died and was buried. [23] In Hades, where he was in torment, he looked up and saw Abraham far away, with Lazarus by his side. [24] So he called to him, 'Father Abraham, have pity on me and send Lazarus to dip the tip of his finger in water and cool my tongue, because I am in agony in this fire.'
>
> [25] "But Abraham replied, 'Son, remember that in your lifetime you received your good things, while Lazarus received bad things, but now he is comforted here and you are in agony. [26] And besides all this, between us and you a great chasm has been set in place, so that those who want to go from here to you cannot, nor can anyone cross over from there to us.'

> [27] "He answered, 'Then I beg you, father, send Lazarus to my family, [28] for I have five brothers. Let him warn them, so that they will not also come to this place of torment.'
>
> [29] "Abraham replied, 'They have Moses and the Prophets; let them listen to them.'
>
> [30] "'No, father Abraham,' he said, 'but if someone from the dead goes to them, they will repent.'
>
> [31] "He said to him, 'If they do not listen to Moses and the Prophets, they will not be convinced even if someone rises from the dead.'" (Luke 16:19–31)

Jesus taught in Luke 16:19–31 that Jews who loved money and rejected the Scriptures (Moses and the Prophets) would not believe in the Scriptures because somebody came back from the dead and preached to them.[14] In this parable, a beggar named Lazarus ate scraps from the home of an unnamed rich man. Lazarus died and went to the heavenly paradise (Abraham's side) while the rich man died and went to Hades. The rich man asked Father Abraham if Lazarus could use his finger to bring a few drops of comforting water from paradise to Hades, but Abraham said that a fixed chasm between the two places would prevent that. Then, the rich men asked Abraham if Lazarus could rise from the dead and warn the rich man's living brothers about Hades. However, Abraham said that if they reject the Scriptures now, then seeing somebody come back from the dead would not change their mind.

The context of the heavenly paradise and Hades is an interim place of rewards and punishments. For example, Luke 10:8–15 teaches about a future judgment day while 16:19–31 portrays some level of rewards and punishments during death before judgment day.

In Luke 17:1–2, Jesus taught that if anybody causes another to stumble into sin, then they would be better off if he were "thrown into the sea with a millstone tied around their neck than to cause one of these little ones to stumble."[15]

Jesus taught about the kingdom in Luke 17:20–37:

> [20] Once, on being asked by the Pharisees when the kingdom of God would come, Jesus replied, "The coming of the kingdom of

---

14. "Moses and the Prophets" were the Scriptures for many Jews in the first century AD.

15. A millstone is a large stone used for milling.

God is not something that can be observed, ²¹ nor will people say, 'Here it is,' or 'There it is,' because the kingdom of God is in your midst."

²² Then he said to his disciples, "The time is coming when you will long to see one of the days of the Son of Man, but you will not see it. ²³ People will tell you, 'There he is!' or 'Here he is!' Do not go running off after them. ²⁴ For the Son of Man in his day will be like the lightning, which flashes and lights up the sky from one end to the other. ²⁵ But first he must suffer many things and be rejected by this generation.

²⁶ "Just as it was in the days of Noah, so also will it be in the days of the Son of Man. ²⁷ People were eating, drinking, marrying and being given in marriage up to the day Noah entered the ark. Then the flood came and destroyed them all.

²⁸ "It was the same in the days of Lot. People were eating and drinking, buying and selling, planting and building. ²⁹ But the day Lot left Sodom, fire and sulfur rained down from heaven and destroyed them all.

³⁰ "It will be just like this on the day the Son of Man is revealed. ³¹ On that day no one who is on the housetop, with possessions inside, should go down to get them. Likewise, no one in the field should go back for anything. ³² Remember Lot's wife! ³³ Whoever tries to keep their life will lose it, and whoever loses their life will preserve it. ³⁴ I tell you, on that night two people will be in one bed; one will be taken and the other left. ³⁵ Two women will be grinding grain together; one will be taken and the other left."

³⁷ "Where, Lord?" they asked.

He replied, "Where there is a dead body, there the vultures will gather." (Luke 17:20–37)[16]

In Luke 17:20–37, Jesus taught that the kingdom of God was both an immediate and future reality. The kingdom was already in the "midst" of his audience, and there would be a future time when the Son of Man would return like lightning that lights up the sky. The return is also associated with sudden judgment analogous to the flood in days of Noah and the destruction of Sodom. Additionally, two people close to each other might have a completely different experience of the judgment: (1) two

---

16. The NIV excludes verse 17:36, which does not appear in the earliest known manuscripts.

people could lie in the same bed while only one of them suffers from the judgment; (2) two people could work side by side at the same job while only one of them suffers from the judgment.

In Luke 19:11–27, Jesus told a parable where a servant gets punished for not using his resources while enemies of a newly appointed king are killed.

In Luke 19:41–44, Jesus warned about a day when enemies would surround and destroy Jerusalem:[17]

> [41] As he [Jesus] approached Jerusalem and saw the city, he wept over it [42] and said, "If you, even you, had only known on this day what would bring you peace—but now it is hidden from your eyes. [43] The days will come upon you when your enemies will build an embankment against you and encircle you and hem you in on every side. [44] They will dash you to the ground, you and the children within your walls. They will not leave one stone on another, because you did not recognize the time of God's coming to you." (Luke 19:41–44)

In Luke 20:9–16, Jesus taught a parable where tenants of a vineyard tried to take possession of the vineyard by killing the son of the owner. Then, the owner "will come and kill those tenants and give the vineyard to others."

In Luke 20:42–43, Jesus quoted Psalm 110:1 while declaring (1) himself the Messiah and (2) that his enemies would be a footstool for his feet.

In Luke 20:45–47, Jesus taught that religious leaders who relish pomp and public respect but devour the estates of widows would face the most severe punishment.

Luke 21:5–38, The Olivet Prophecy (Discourse)

> [5] Some of his disciples were remarking about how the temple was adorned with beautiful stones and with gifts dedicated to God. But Jesus said, [6] "As for what you see here, the time will come when not one stone will be left on another; every one of them will be thrown down."
>
> [7] "Teacher," they asked, "when will these things happen? And what will be the sign that they are about to take place?"

---

17. See Luke 21:5–38.

⁸ He replied: "Watch out that you are not deceived. For many will come in my name, claiming, 'I am he,' and, 'The time is near.' Do not follow them. ⁹ When you hear of wars and uprisings, do not be frightened. These things must happen first, but the end will not come right away."

¹⁰ Then he said to them: "Nation will rise against nation, and kingdom against kingdom. ¹¹ There will be great earthquakes, famines and pestilences in various places, and fearful events and great signs from heaven.

¹² "But before all this, they will seize you and persecute you. They will hand you over to synagogues and put you in prison, and you will be brought before kings and governors, and all on account of my name. ¹³ And so you will bear testimony to me. ¹⁴ But make up your mind not to worry beforehand how you will defend yourselves. ¹⁵ For I will give you words and wisdom that none of your adversaries will be able to resist or contradict. ¹⁶ You will be betrayed even by parents, brothers and sisters, relatives and friends, and they will put some of you to death. ¹⁷ Everyone will hate you because of me. ¹⁸ But not a hair of your head will perish. ¹⁹ Stand firm, and you will win life.

²⁰ "When you see Jerusalem being surrounded by armies, you will know that its desolation is near. ²¹ Then let those who are in Judea flee to the mountains, let those in the city get out, and let those in the country not enter the city. ²² For this is the time of punishment in fulfillment of all that has been written. ²³ How dreadful it will be in those days for pregnant women and nursing mothers! There will be great distress in the land and wrath against this people. ²⁴ They will fall by the sword and will be taken as prisoners to all the nations. Jerusalem will be trampled on by the Gentiles until the times of the Gentiles are fulfilled.

²⁵ "There will be signs in the sun, moon and stars. On the earth, nations will be in anguish and perplexity at the roaring and tossing of the sea. ²⁶ People will faint from terror, apprehensive of what is coming on the world, for the heavenly bodies will be shaken. ²⁷ At that time they will see the Son of Man coming in a cloud with power and great glory. ²⁸ When these things begin to take place, stand up and lift up your heads, because your redemption is drawing near."

²⁹ He told them this parable: "Look at the fig tree and all the trees. ³⁰ When they sprout leaves, you can see for yourselves and know

> that summer is near. ³¹ Even so, when you see these things happening, you know that the kingdom of God is near.
>
> ³² "Truly I tell you, this generation will certainly not pass away until all these things have happened. ³³ Heaven and earth will pass away, but my words will never pass away.
>
> ³⁴ "Be careful, or your hearts will be weighed down with carousing, drunkenness and the anxieties of life, and that day will close on you suddenly like a trap. ³⁵ For it will come on all those who live on the face of the whole earth. ³⁶ Be always on the watch, and pray that you may be able to escape all that is about to happen, and that you may be able to stand before the Son of Man."
>
> ³⁷ Each day Jesus was teaching at the temple, and each evening he went out to spend the night on the hill called the Mount of Olives, ³⁸ and all the people came early in the morning to hear him at the temple. (Luke 21:5–38)

Luke 21:5–38, Matthew 24, and Mark 13 are parallel accounts called the Olivet prophecy (discourse). Jesus spoke the prophecy from the Jerusalem Mount of Olives during the week before his death by crucifixion.[18]

Luke's Olivet prophecy technically started with Luke 21:8 while 21:5–7 set the stage. In verse 21:5, disciples remark about the beauty of the Jerusalem temple. For example, around 19 BC, the Roman client king Herod began to expand the temple. The expanded temple built with cream-colored stones and gold plates stood ninety feet high. People from miles away saw the sun glisten off the cream stones and gold. In verse 21:6, Jesus announced the eventual leveling of every stone used to build the magnificent temple. Then, in verse 21:7, the disciples asked when this will happen and what sign would precede this event.

In Luke 21:8–11, Jesus began his prophecy. He warned his disciples about signs to come: (1) people claiming to be Christ while declaring the end, (2) wars, (3) great earthquakes, (4) famines, (5) pestilence, (6), fearful events, and (7) signs from heaven.

In Luke 21:12–19, Jesus said that before these signs, enemies would seize and persecute the disciples; even relatives would betray the disciples to death. On the bright side, persecutors would bring disciples

---

18. Jesus may have spoken about this prophecy on more than one occasion during this week, which might account for the differences in prophecy between Matthew, Mark, and Luke.

before kings and governors, which would result in the disciples testifying on behalf of Jesus.

In Luke 21:20–24, Jesus warned about the future desolation of Jerusalem. Divine wrath would cause the desolation. The desolation would be a dreadful, great distress. Armies surrounding Jerusalem would indicate that its desolation is near. Then, gentiles would trample Jerusalem. They would kill and imprison many Jews in Jerusalem.

In Luke 21:25–28, Jesus taught about the signs of his return. The sky will show signs. People from all nations will feel terror from the signs. At that time, the entire world "will see the Son of Man coming in a cloud with power and great glory."

In Luke 21:29–33, Jesus taught: (1) these signs indicate that the kingdom of God is near; (2) the generation of Jesus would see all of the signs.

In Luke 21:34–36, Jesus warned his disciples that his return would close in like a sudden trap for those who weigh down their hearts with things like carousing, drunkenness, and the anxieties of life. But those who carefully watch and pray may stand before the Son of Man when he returns.

Luke 21:37–38 says that Jesus taught each day in the temple and spent each night on the hill called the Mount of Olives.

Jesus capitalized on his disciples remarking about the magnificence of the temple by using that to set the stage for prophesying about the persecution of disciples, the desolation of Jerusalem, and the Lord's return. Also, Jesus said that his generation would see the signs for the desolation of Jerusalem and the Lord's return, which as stated earlier include the persecution of disciples, people claiming to be Christ while declaring the end, wars, great earthquakes, famines, pestilence, fearful events, and signs from heaven. Additionally, disciples saw examples of all these signs by the AD 70 destruction of Jerusalem, which is what Jesus meant by saying, "This generation will certainly not pass away until all these things have happened." Examples of these signs include persecution against Paul helping him to share the gospel with various political rulers,[19] false prophets described as antichrists,[20] false prophets instigating rebellion against Rome in the first Jewish-Roman war leading to the destruction

---

19. See Acts 21:27—28:31.
20. See 1 John 4:1–3.

of Jerusalem,[21] the earthquake freeing Paul and Silas from prison,[22] the AD 62 Pompeii earthquake, the famine prophesied by Agabus,[23] and various solar eclipses. These signs such as persecution against Christian disciples, false prophets, wars, earthquakes, and famines by no means ended with the horrific AD 70 destruction of Jerusalem, but examples of all the signs were clearly seen by then. Additionally, Jesus concluded the prophecy by saying that those who are weighed down by sin and do not watch and pray would be subject to sudden judgment by his return.

Concerning the conditional nature of prophecy, the judgment Christ spoke against Jerusalem was conditional. Regardless that Jerusalem literally faced attack from armies and great desolation in AD 70, Rome never would have surrounded and destroyed Jerusalem if all the respective Jewish leaders and seditious rebels decided to follow Christ. Such a conversion of the Jewish leaders and seditious rebels would have resulted in no political rebellion against Rome, leaving Rome with no rebellion to crush.

Sum of Luke on Imagery of Judgment

Luke describes judgment as annihilating fire, purging fire, destruction, banishment to the Abyss, proportional to how one judges, proportional to the amount of disobedience, falling from heaven, accumulative judgment, thrown into hell, disowned by God, cut to pieces, paying the last penny of debt, perishing, banishment, weeping, gnashing of teeth, surprising twists, military attacks, and desolation. The imagery looks diverse and fearful.

SELECTIONS FROM MARK ON JUDGMENT

Outline of Mark on Judgment

Imagery of judgment in Mark includes:

1. A man possessed by an impure spirit (demon) cried out, "What do you want with us, Jesus of Nazareth? Have you come to destroy us?" (Mark 1:23–24)

---

21. See Josephus, Book 6, chapter 5.
22. See Acts 16:26.
23. See Acts 11:28.

2. Jesus commanded the demon to silence and come out of the man. (Mark 1:25)

3. Jesus warns Jewish leaders that God forgives all sins and blasphemies, "but whoever blasphemes against the Holy Spirit will never be forgiven; they are guilty of an eternal sin." (Mark 3:22–30)

4. A deranged man possessed by many demons approached Jesus near a lake and shouted, "What do you want with me, Jesus, Son of the Most High God? In God's name don't torture me!" (Mark 5:1–8)

5. Jesus said if people are ashamed of him and his words, then he will be ashamed of them when he returns with his Father's glory and the angels. (Mark 8:38)

6. Jesus called his generation "unbelieving" and questioned how long he would stay with them and put up with them. (Mark 9:19)

7. Jesus said if anybody causes a believer to stumble into sin, they would be better off then "if a large millstone were hung around their neck and they were thrown into the sea." (Mark 9:42)

8. Jesus said if your hand causes you to sin, then "cut it off" because it is better to live maimed than with two hands and go to hell (Gehenna) "where the fire never goes out." (Mark 9:43)

9. Jesus said if your foot causes you to sin, then "cut it off" because it is better to live "crippled than to have two feet and be thrown into hell." (Mark 9:45)

10. Jesus said to pluck out your eye if it causes you to sin because it is better to enter the kingdom of God with one eye "than to have two eyes and be thrown into hell, where 'the worms that eat them do not die, and the fire is not quenched.'" (Mark 9:47–48)

11. Jesus entered the temple courts and drove out the buyers and sellers; he overturned the tables of the money exchangers and the benches of the dove sellers; he said, "Is it not written: 'My house will be called a house of prayer for all nations'? But you have made it 'a den of robbers.'" (Mark 11:15–17)

12. Tenants of a vineyard tried to take possession of the vineyard by killing the son of the owner; then the owner "will come and kill those tenants and give the vineyard to others." (Mark 12:7–9)

13. Jesus said, "The Lord said to my Lord: 'Sit at my right hand until I put your enemies under your feet.'" (Mark 12:36)

14. Jesus said religious leaders who relish pomp and public respect but devour the estates of widows will face the most severe punishment. (Mark 12:38–40)

15. Jesus said, "Not one stone here will be left on another; every one will be thrown down." (Mark 13:2)

16. Jesus said, "Those will be days of distress unequaled from the beginning, when God created the world, until now—and never to be equaled again." (Mark 13:19)

17. The sun and moon will darken while stars and heavenly bodies fall from the sky. (Mark 13:24–25)

18. "Woe to that man who betrays the Son of Man! It would be better for him if he had not been born." (Mark 14:21)

The imagery of judgment in Mark includes destruction, shame, torture, unforgiveness, a person thrown into the sea with a large stone tied to his neck, a person thrown into fire that never quenches and eaten by worms that never die, killing murderers, the most severe punishment, the greatest distress in history, and a person better off if never born. Also, the criteria for judgment in Mark includes possessing humans, blaspheming the Holy Spirit, feeling ashamed of Jesus and his words, causing others to sin, sinning with your hands, sinning with your feet, sinning with your eyes, greedy commercialization of religious services, killing the Son of God, relishing pomp and respect while greedily manipulating the estates of widows, and betraying the Son of God.

Mark 13, The Olivet Prophecy

Mark's Olivet prophecy has both similarities to and differences from Luke's Olivet prophecy. The differences in the parallel versions of the Olivet prophecy may involve that Jesus met with his disciples on the Mount of Olives every evening during the last week before Jesus died by crucifixion.[24] All versions of the prophecy include a prologue that began with a discussion between Jesus and his disciples about the temple in Jerusalem:

---

24. See Luke 21:37–38.

> ¹ As he [Jesus] was leaving the temple, one of his disciples said to him, "Look, Teacher! What massive stones! What magnificent buildings!"
>
> ² "Do you see all these great buildings?" replied Jesus. "Not one stone here will be left on another; every one will be thrown down."
>
> ³ As Jesus was sitting on the Mount of Olives opposite the temple, Peter, James, John and Andrew asked him privately, ⁴ "Tell us, when will these things happen? And what will be the sign that they are all about to be fulfilled?" (Mark 13:1–4)

As mentioned earlier, the temple stood ninety feet high with glistening cream-colored stones and gold plates while the disciples pointed out the magnificence of the temple to Jesus. Then, Jesus and his closest disciples went to the nearby Mount of Olives.[25] They asked Jesus about the timing of the destruction of the Jerusalem temple and the sign that would warn about the destruction. Then, Jesus spoke his famous prophecy:

> ⁵ Jesus said to them: "Watch out that no one deceives you. ⁶ Many will come in my name, claiming, 'I am he,' and will deceive many. ⁷ When you hear of wars and rumors of wars, do not be alarmed. Such things must happen, but the end is still to come. ⁸ Nation will rise against nation, and kingdom against kingdom. There will be earthquakes in various places, and famines. These are the beginning of birth pains.
>
> ⁹ "You must be on your guard. You will be handed over to the local councils and flogged in the synagogues. On account of me you will stand before governors and kings as witnesses to them. ¹⁰ And the gospel must first be preached to all nations. ¹¹ Whenever you are arrested and brought to trial, do not worry beforehand about what to say. Just say whatever is given you at the time, for it is not you speaking, but the Holy Spirit.
>
> ¹² "Brother will betray brother to death, and a father his child. Children will rebel against their parents and have them put to death. ¹³ All men will hate you because of me, but he who stands firm to the end will be saved.

---

25. Matthew and Mark both say that Jesus sat at the Mount of Olives while Luke never mentions the Mount of Olives as the setting for this prophecy.

[14] "When you see 'the abomination that causes desolation' standing where it does not belong—let the reader understand—then let those who are in Judea flee to the mountains. [15] Let no one on the roof of his house go down or enter the house to take anything out. [16] Let no one in the field go back to get his cloak. [17] How dreadful it will be in those days for pregnant women and nursing mothers! [18] Pray that this will not take place in winter, [19] because those will be days of distress unequaled from the beginning, when God created the world, until now—and never to be equaled again. [20] If the Lord had not cut short those days, no one would survive. But for the sake of the elect, whom he has chosen, he has shortened them. [21] At that time if anyone says to you, 'Look, here is the Christ!' or, 'Look, there he is!' do not believe it. [22] For false Christs and false prophets will appear and perform signs and miracles to deceive the elect—if that were possible. [23] So be on your guard; I have told you everything ahead of time.

[24] "But in those days, following that distress,

" 'the sun will be darkened,
and the moon will not give its light;

[25] the stars will fall from the sky,
and the heavenly bodies will be shaken.'

[26] "At that time men will see the Son of Man coming in clouds with great power and glory. [27] And he will send his angels and gather his elect from the four winds, from the ends of the earth to the ends of the heavens.

[28] "Now learn this lesson from the fig tree: As soon as its twigs get tender and its leaves come out, you know that summer is near. [29] Even so, when you see these things happening, you know that it is near, right at the door. [30] I tell you the truth, this generation will certainly not pass away until all these things have happened. [31] Heaven and earth will pass away, but my words will never pass away.

[32] "No one knows about that day or hour, not even the angels in heaven, nor the Son, but only the Father. [33] Be on guard! Be alert! You do not know when that time will come. [34] It's like a man going away: He leaves his house and puts his servants in charge, each with his assigned task, and tells the one at the door to keep watch.

[35] "Therefore keep watch because you do not know when the owner of the house will come back—whether in the evening, or at midnight, or when the rooster crows, or at dawn. [36] If he comes suddenly, do not let him find you sleeping. [37] What I say to you, I say to everyone: 'Watch!'" (Mark 13:5–37)

In Mark 13:5–8, Jesus began the prophecy by warning his disciples about (1) many deceivers claiming to be the Messiah, (2) wars and rumors of wars, (3) imprisonments, (4) earthquakes, and (5) famines. He also compared these events to birth pains that signified the end.

In Mark 13:9–11, Jesus encouraged his disciples by saying that the Holy Spirit would give them words to speak when persecutors arrested and imprisoned them. Jesus also said that his disciples would preach the gospel to all nations before the end.

In Mark 13:12–23, Jesus predicted the worst of times on earth: (1) all people hating his disciples including ungodly relatives betraying godly relatives to death, (2) "the abomination that causes desolation," (3) the greatest distress in history, and (4) the rise of false Christs and false prophets who perform miracles while trying to deceive believers.

In Mark 13:24–27, Jesus said that after the greatest distress there would be great signs in the sky and then he would return with great power and glory, while his angels gather the elect (believers) from the ends of the earth.

In Mark 13:28–31, Jesus taught his disciples to be watchful for the signs that would indicate his return.

In Mark 13:32–37, Jesus taught believers must keep vigilance and faithfulness until the return of the Lord because nobody but the Father knows when the Lord will return. This implied an imminent return of the Lord after the fulfillment of the signs in the Olivet prophecy.

Mark 13:30 said that the first generation of Christians would see "all these things." The context of "all these things" refers to the question in 13:4: "Tell us, when will these things happen? And what will be the sign that they are all about to be fulfilled?" Jesus predicted in verse 13:30 that the first generation of Christians would see examples of all the events that *precede* the return of Jesus. These examples included the spread of the gospel in the Roman Empire, the famine prophesied by Agabus in Acts 11:28, the AD 70 Jerusalem famine, the earthquake in Acts 16:26, the AD 62 Pompeii earthquake, and the AD 70 destruction of Jerusalem.[26]

The first Jewish-Roman war ending in AD 70 played a major role in the fulfillment of the Olivet prophecy. As discussed in chapter 9, in

---

26. Full preterists claim that "all these things" include the return of Jesus and say that Jesus returned in AD 70 during the destruction of Jerusalem. However, full preterists reject that the Bible teaches about a visible return of Jesus.

AD 70, General Titus and his army surrounded Jerusalem, slaughtered hundreds of thousands of Jews, heaped and burned many dead Jews around the Jewish altar, and destroyed the entire Jewish temple by fire except parts of the retaining walls. This war initially fulfilled the prophecy in Mark 13:2, which said that not one temple stone would be left on another. This war also foreshadowed "the abomination that causes desolation" in Mark 13:24.

As discussed in chapter 9, the original "abomination that causes desolation" specifically referred to Antiochus Epiphanes in 168 BC making sacrifices to Zeus on the Jewish altar. However, in a broader sense, the desolation included Antiochus and his army capturing Jerusalem while slaughtering tens of thousands of Jews before he made the sacrifices to Zeus. Similarly, the broader meaning of Mark's desolation includes Luke's prediction of armies surrounding and trampling Jerusalem. Also, in all the synoptic versions of the Olivet prophecy, Jesus referred to the desolation by Antiochus as a prefiguration of a future event. Also, the AD 70 destruction of Jerusalem looks like a fulfillment for that prophecy.

However, the AD 70 destruction of Jerusalem never ushered in the return of Jesus. Also, Mark 13:19 said that the desolation would be the greatest distress in the history of the world, never to be equaled, which referred to Daniel 12:1. Nevertheless, horrific events in the twentieth century such as Adolph Hitler's holocaust suggest that the horrors of AD 70 were not literally the greatest distress in history, never to be equaled. Likewise, the AD 70 destruction of Jerusalem was a fulfillment of the prophecy about the abomination that causes desolation, but it was a prefiguration of the final fulfillment.[27]

Jesus also assured his disciples that he would return after the great distress and completely establish his kingdom on earth. Finally, Jesus paradoxically warned his disciples to watch for the signs of his sudden return while encouraging vigilance and faithfulness.

SELECTIONS FROM MATTHEW ON JUDGMENT

Matthew 3:1–12 and Judgment by Fire

Matthew 3:1–12 parallels Luke 3:1–19 discussed earlier. For example, Matthew quotes John the Baptist using imagery of judgment that shows

---

27. Chapters 12 and 14 discuss the implications of conditional futurism and the great distress.

an ax ready to cut down unproductive trees at their roots before the trees are thrown into fire and end from annihilation. Also, Matthew quotes John portraying believers as wheat on the Messiah's threshing floor while the Messiah uses his winnowing fork to separate the wheat grain from its chaff. The chaff gets thrown into "unquenchable fire." Likewise, John in both Matthew and Luke used imagery of the fires of Gehenna both annihilating unproductive trees and purging the chaff from wheat grains. Also, Jesus in Matthew used the word *hell* (Gehenna) seven times,[28] and he referred to the fires of Gehenna in four other verses.[29]

Matthew on Proportions of Punishment

Matthew also parallels Luke with teaching about differing proportions of punishment: Matthew 5:25–26 illustrates judgment with a civil judge sentencing somebody to prison until they pay the last penny;[30] Matthew 6:37–38 teaches that people are judged according to the proportion that they judge others;[31] Matthew 11:20–24 prophesies that some towns will face a more severe judgment than others based on the amount of divine revelation that has been rejected;[32] Matthew 16:27 says that Jesus will return with his Father's glory and reward each person according to what they have done, good or bad.

Matthew 7:13–14 and 8:11–12

In Matthew 7:13–14, Jesus directed his audience to enter the "narrow gate" and warned that a wide gate leads to destruction. Also, many enter the wide gate to destruction while only a few would find the narrow gate that leads to life. Additionally, these verses partially parallel Luke 13:22–30 earlier in this chapter where Jesus warned that only a few Jews of his generation would find the "narrow door" and enjoy the end-time feast of God.

In Matthew 8:11–12, Jesus declared that many gentiles from around the world will enjoy the great end-time feast in the kingdom of God

---

28. See Matthew 5:22, 5:29, 5:30, 10:28, 18:9, 23:15, and 23:33. Also, see earlier references in Luke 12:5 and Mark 9:43, 9:45, and 9:47.

29. See Matthew 7:19, 13:40, 18:8, and 25:41.

30. See earlier reference to Luke 12:58–59.

31. See earlier reference to Luke 6:37–38.

32. See earlier reference to Luke 10:8–15.

while many Jews will miss the feast and be thrown into "darkness" while many in the darkness would weep and angrily gnash their teeth.[33] These verses also partially parallel Luke 13:22–30 where Jesus warned that only a few Jews of his generation would enjoy the end-time feast of God while many gentiles from around the world would enjoy the great feast.

Matthew 22:1–14 and 23:1–39

Jesus taught a parable in Matthew 22:1–14:[34] A king sent servants to invite guests to his son's wedding banquet. Some invitees ignored the king's invitations while others killed the servants who gave the invitations. The king felt enraged by the responses and sent an army to destroy the city that ignored and killed his servants. Then, the king sent his servants to invite anyone that the servants could find on the streets, and the wedding hall filled with guests. During the banquet, the king visited the guests and saw a man without wedding clothes. The king asked him how he got in without wedding clothes, but the man had no answer. Then, the king told his servants, "Tie him hand and foot, and throw him outside, into the darkness, where there will be weeping and gnashing of teeth. For many are invited, but few are chosen."

This parable teaches about the conditions in God's covenant such as accepting God's invitation. This verse also describes punishment in "darkness" instead of the fires of hell. Additionally, the punishment of being tied hand and foot and thrown in darkness refers to imagery in 1 Enoch 10:4–6.

Matthew 23

In Matthew 23, Jesus spoke many judgments to Jewish leaders in Jerusalem because of their hypocrisy. He concluded the judgments in Matthew 23:33–39:

> [33] "You snakes! You brood of vipers! How will you escape being condemned to hell? [34] Therefore I am sending you prophets and sages and teachers. Some of them you will kill and crucify; others you will flog in your synagogues and pursue from town to town. [35] And so upon you will come all the righteous blood

---

33. Matthew 8:11 uses the phrase *kingdom of heaven* as a synonym for "kingdom of God."

34. See earlier reference to Luke 14:16–24.

that has been shed on earth, from the blood of righteous Abel to the blood of Zechariah son of Berekiah, whom you murdered between the temple and the altar. ³⁶ Truly I tell you, all this will come on this generation.

³⁷ "Jerusalem, Jerusalem, you who kill the prophets and stone those sent to you, how often I have longed to gather your children together, as a hen gathers her chicks under her wings, and you were not willing. ³⁸ Look, your house is left to you desolate. ³⁹ For I tell you, you will not see me again until you say, 'Blessed is he who comes in the name of the Lord.'" (Matthew 23:33–39)

Jesus warned the leaders that they faced condemnation in hell because of their hypocrisy. Also, Jesus said that he would send them prophets to turn them from their hypocrisy, and Jesus predicted that the leaders would persecute the prophets, killing some of them. Then, Jesus proclaimed longing to see the Jews in Jerusalem turn to the Lord while he warned that Jerusalem would suffer judgment resulting in desolation. Additionally, Jesus pronounced that his generation of Jews that rejected the Lord would face an accumulation of judgment for all prophets who had previously been persecuted.

Matthew 24, The Olivet Prophecy

Matthew 24:1–35 closely parallels Mark 13:1–31. And Matthew 24:36–51 includes speeches recorded in Mark 13:32–36, Luke 12:42–46, and Luke 17:26–27.

In Matthew 24:1–2, the disciples remarked to Jesus about the buildings in the Jerusalem temple and Jesus said that all of the stones in the temple walls would be thrown to the ground.

In Matthew 24:3, Jesus and his disciples sat on the Mount of Olives while the disciples asked, "When will this happen, and what will be the sign of your coming and of the end of the age?"

In Matthew 24:4–8, Jesus began the prophecy by warning his disciples about (1) many deceivers claiming to be the Messiah, (2) wars and rumors of wars, (3) famines, and (4) earthquakes. He told his disciples to remain unalarmed during wars and rumors of wars. He also compared these events to birth pains, signifying the end of human history.

In Matthew 24:9–14, Jesus prophesied: his disciples would face persecution and death; all nations would hate the disciples; many false prophets would deceive many people; the increase in wickedness would result in people's love growing cold; but those who stand firm to the end would be saved. Also, the gospel of God's kingdom will be preached to all nations before the end comes.

In Matthew 24:15–21, Jesus warned about seeing the "the abomination that causes desolation" standing in the holy place, as prophesied by Daniel. When the abomination is seen, then those in Judea need to flee as fast as possible. That time will be dreadful for pregnant women and nursing mothers. Moreover, "there will be great distress, unequaled from the beginning of the world until now—and never to be equaled again."

In Matthew 24:22–28, Jesus said that the days of the great distress will be shortened or nobody would survive them. Also, Jesus warned that during the great distress false Christs and false prophets would perform miracles and try to deceive the disciples. Additionally, Jesus said that nobody should try visiting or believing anybody else who claims to be the Christ while Christ clarified that his return would be as clear as lightning in the sky going from east to west.

In Matthew 24:29–31, Jesus said that after the greatest distress there would be great signs in the sky and then he would return with great power and glory, while his angels gather the disciples from the ends of the earth.

In Matthew 24:32–35, Jesus taught his disciples to be watchful for the signs that would indicate his return.

In Matthew 24:36–39, Jesus analogized the return of the Lord to the flood in the days of Noah. In those days, everybody lived a carefree life until the great flood suddenly took most people away in judgment.

In Matthew 24:40–41, Jesus used analogies that describe people working together while suddenly some are taken away in judgment while others are left behind.

In Matthew 24:42–44, Jesus encouraged vigilance while ironically comparing the return of the Lord to a thief in the night. For example, if a homeowner would know when a thief would try to break into a home, then the homeowner would be vigilant and stop the thief from breaking into the house. Inversely, if a believer is always vigilant, then the believer will be ready for the sudden return of the Lord.

In Matthew 24:45–51, Jesus described the options of wisdom versus negligence for a servant in charge of his master's household while the master left for a journey. If the servant is wise, then the servant will always take care of the household including the other servants. When the master returns, he will reward the wise servant. But if the servant neglects his duties, gets drunk, and beats the other servants, then the master will send him to judgment.

Matthew 25:1–13, The Parable of Ten Maidens

Matthew 25:1–13 also encourages vigilance while waiting for the return of the Lord. In this parable, Jesus said that ten virgin maidens planned to escort a bridegroom to his wedding. Five of the maidens were foolish and took their lamps with no oil while the other five maidens were wise and took oil with their lamps. The bridegroom suddenly approached at midnight. The foolish maidens could not get oil for their lamps and escort the bridegroom while the five wise maidens lit their lamps and escorted the bridegroom. The foolish maidens had left to purchase some oil and arrived late for the wedding. When they knocked on the door to get into the wedding, the bridegroom said, "I don't know you."

Matthew 25:14–30, The Parable of the Talents

Matthew 25:14–30 encourages faithful use of resources while waiting for the return of the Lord. Jesus compared his return to the master of a house leaving for a journey. The master organized three of his servants. He gave the first servant five million dollars ("five talents of money"),[35] the second two million dollars, and third servant one million dollars, each according to his abilities. The first servant used his five million dollars to earn another five million dollars. The second servant used his two million dollars to earn another two million dollars. However, the third servant buried his million dollars into the ground to keep it safe. When the master returned, he greatly rewarded the first two servants. But he told the third servant that he should have at least put the money in the bank to earn interest. And he said, "Throw that worthless servant outside, into the darkness, where there will be weeping and gnashing of teeth."

Matthew 25:31–46, The Sheep and the Goats

> [31] "When the Son of Man comes in his glory, and all the angels with him, he will sit on his throne in heavenly glory. [32] All the nations will be gathered before him, and he will separate the

---

35. The original biblical text refers to talents of gold, while a talent weighs ninety-four pounds (forty-three kilograms).

people one from another as a shepherd separates the sheep from the goats. ³³ He will put the sheep on his right and the goats on his left.

³⁴ "Then the King will say to those on his right, 'Come, you who are blessed by my Father; take your inheritance, the kingdom prepared for you since the creation of the world. ³⁵ For I was hungry and you gave me something to eat, I was thirsty and you gave me something to drink, I was a stranger and you invited me in, ³⁶ I needed clothes and you clothed me, I was sick and you looked after me, I was in prison and you came to visit me.'

³⁷ "Then the righteous will answer him, 'Lord, when did we see you hungry and feed you, or thirsty and give you something to drink? ³⁸ When did we see you a stranger and invite you in, or needing clothes and clothe you? ³⁹ When did we see you sick or in prison and go to visit you?'

⁴⁰ "The King will reply, 'I tell you the truth, whatever you did for one of the least of these brothers of mine, you did for me.'

⁴¹ "Then he will say to those on his left, 'Depart from me, you who are cursed, into the eternal fire prepared for the devil and his angels. ⁴² For I was hungry and you gave me nothing to eat, I was thirsty and you gave me nothing to drink, ⁴³ I was a stranger and you did not invite me in, I needed clothes and you did not clothe me, I was sick and in prison and you did not look after me.'

⁴⁴ "They also will answer, 'Lord, when did we see you hungry or thirsty or a stranger or needing clothes or sick or in prison, and did not help you?'

⁴⁵ "He will reply, 'I tell you the truth, whatever you did not do for one of the least of these, you did not do for me.'

⁴⁶ "Then they will go away to eternal punishment, but the righteous to eternal life." (Matthew 25:31–46)

Matthew concludes his compilation of end-time prophecy with Jesus describing a symbolic picture about judgment of the nations during the return of the Lord. Jesus compares all people in the nations of the earth to sheep and goats. After he returns, the sheep line up at his right and the goats line up on his left. Then, the Lord will invite the sheep into his kingdom because they helped the Lord by helping his brothers when they were needy. The Lord will banish the goats into eternal fire prepared for the devil and his angels because the goats never helped the

Lord by helping his brothers when they were needy. In sum, the unhelpful, cursed humans go away to eternal punishment and the helpful, righteous humans go to eternal life. Likewise, the requirements for eternal life include helpfulness to others.

The pictures of "eternal punishment" and "eternal life" compare everlasting destinies based on helpfulness or unhelpfulness during earthly life. Also, the imagery of eternal punishment includes a permanent banishment from God and retribution in everlasting fire for (1) the devil, (2) the devil's angels, and (3) humans who neglected the needs of others. This imagery of everlasting punishment in fire referred to Isaiah 66:24 and the pseudonymous 1 Enoch.

Sum of Matthew on the Imagery of Judgment

Matthew includes most of the imagery of judgment found in Luke and Mark: annihilating fire, purging fire, destruction, proportional to how one judges, proportional to the amount of disobedience, accumulation of judgment, thrown into hell, disowned by God, cut to pieces, paying the last penny of debt, perishing, banishment, weeping, gnashing of teeth, surprising twists, military attacks, and desolation. Matthew also adds the imagery of punishment in darkness.

NOTES FROM JOHN ON JUDGMENT

John summarizes important points about judgment in verses 3:16, 5:22–23, 5:28–29, and 14:1–3:

1. John 3:16 portrays all humans as destined to perish while belief in the Son of God (Jesus) would lead instead to eternal life.

2. John 5:22–23 teaches that Jesus is the end-time judge who shares equal honor with the Father.

3. John 5:28–29 teaches about conditions for the end-time resurrection: those who did good will rise to life while those who did bad will rise to condemnation.

4. John 14:1–3 proclaims the end-time fulfillment of Jesus returning to take his believers to be with him and the Father.

TENSIONS OF JUDGMENT IN THE GOSPELS

The teachings of judgment in the Gospels include tensions. These tensions involve judgment proportional to disobedience, an accumulative judgment, and various imagery of judgment in fire.

Luke and Matthew teach about judgment proportional to disobedience and an accumulative judgment for the Jewish leaders contemporary to Jesus. The teaching about an accumulative judgment for leaders that ended up horrifically destroying all Jerusalem in AD 70 appears paradoxical to teaching about judgment proportional to disobedience. In this case, two biblical authors present the same paradox, which indicates that this tension is not merely disharmonious views from different biblical authors. The horrific fate for the general public of Jews in AD 70 Jerusalem appears as more punishment than many individuals deserved while perhaps postmortem judgments would recompense all injustices and judge all according to the proportion of disobedience.

Another tension of judgment in the Gospels includes Matthew teaching about punishment in the fires of hell and punishment in darkness. Postmortem punishments cannot be both literally in the fires of hell and literally in darkness because light from fire dispels darkness. Perhaps this conflict of literal interpretations within the same book of the Bible suggests a figurative interpretation.

Other tension about judgment in the Gospels includes the teaching about judgment proportional to disobedience and a final endless punishment. For example, Matthew describes imagery of a final judgment that banishes unhelpful people forever away from the presence of God and into eternal fire while Matthew also teaches about judgment that is proportional to the level of disobedience. This imagery of final banishment and eternal fire looks like the same level of judgment for multitudes of unhelpful people, regardless if there were many different levels of disobedience in this group of unhelpful people. Perhaps this conflict of imagery in Matthew also suggests a figurative interpretation.

11

Acts

Luke wrote the Gospel according to Luke and the book of Acts for Theophilus. This chapter looks at Acts 1:1–11, 3:1–26, 7:51–60, and 17:29–31.

ACTS 1:1–11

Acts 1:1–11 summarizes the ministry of Jesus to his apostles after his resurrection and describes his ascension to heaven:

> [1] In my former book, Theophilus, I wrote about all that Jesus began to do and to teach [2] until the day he was taken up to heaven, after giving instructions through the Holy Spirit to the apostles he had chosen. [3] After his suffering, he showed himself to these men and gave many convincing proofs that he was alive. He appeared to them over a period of forty days and spoke about the kingdom of God. [4] On one occasion, while he was eating with them, he gave them this command: "Do not leave Jerusalem, but wait for the gift my Father promised, which you have heard me speak about. [5] For John baptized with water, but in a few days you will be baptized with the Holy Spirit."
>
> [6] So when they met together, they asked him, "Lord, are you at this time going to restore the kingdom to Israel?"
>
> [7] He said to them: "It is not for you to know the times or dates the Father has set by his own authority. [8] But you will receive power when the Holy Spirit comes on you; and you will be my witnesses in Jerusalem, and in all Judea and Samaria, and to the ends of the earth."
>
> [9] After he said this, he was taken up before their very eyes, and a cloud hid him from their sight.

> [10] They were looking intently up into the sky as he was going, when suddenly two men dressed in white stood beside them. [11] "Men of Galilee," they said, why do you stand here looking into the sky? This same Jesus, who has been taken from you into heaven, will come back in the same way you have seen him go into heaven." (Acts 1:1-11)

Jesus appeared to his apostles for forty days after his resurrection and taught them about the kingdom of God and the gift of the Holy Spirit. On the fortieth day after his resurrection, an apostle asked Jesus about the timing of God restoring the kingdom to Israel in the messianic age. Jesus said that the fulfillment of restoring the kingdom to Israel would occur at a later time set by the Father, which referred to the unknowable time frame for the return of the Lord according to the Olivet prophecy. Then, Jesus taught about the first phase of the kingdom. The Holy Spirit would empower the apostles for witnessing throughout the earth. Suddenly, Jesus ascended to the sky and disappeared behind a cloud before the eyes of the apostles. Two angels abruptly appeared as men dressed in white. The angels declared that Jesus was taken from them to heaven and would return from heaven in the same way that he left.

The narration of the ascension of Jesus teaches about the two phases of the kingdom. The first phase focuses on Holy Spirit empowered sharing of the gospel throughout the earth. And the second phase begins with the return of the Lord.

ACTS 3

Acts 3 teaches about healing and faith in the name of Jesus Christ, repentance, instigating the return of the Lord, and the conditions for judgment and blessing during the return of the Lord.

In Acts 3:1-10, Peter helped to heal a crippled beggar in the name of Jesus Christ, and many people saw the former cripple walking and praising God with Peter and John in the Jerusalem temple. Then, Acts 3:11-26:

> [11] While the beggar held on to Peter and John, all the people were astonished and came running to them in the place called Solomon's Colonnade. [12] When Peter saw this, he said to them: Men of Israel, why does this surprise you? Why do you stare at us as if by our own power or godliness we had made this man walk? [13] The God of Abraham, Isaac and Jacob, the God of our fathers,

has glorified his servant Jesus. You handed him over to be killed, and you disowned him before Pilate, though he had decided to let him go. [14] You disowned the Holy and Righteous One and asked that a murderer be released to you. [15] You killed the author of life, but God raised him from the dead. We are witnesses of this. [16] By faith in the name of Jesus, this man whom you see and know was made strong. It is Jesus' name and the faith that comes through him that has given this complete healing to him, as you can all see.

[17] "Now, brothers, I know that you acted in ignorance, as did your leaders. [18] But this is how God fulfilled what he had foretold through all the prophets, saying that his Christ would suffer. [19] Repent, then, and turn to God, so that your sins may be wiped out, that times of refreshing may come from the Lord, [20] and that he may send the Christ, who has been appointed for you—even Jesus. [21] He must remain in heaven until the time comes for God to restore everything, as he promised long ago through his holy prophets. [22] For Moses said, 'The Lord your God will raise up for you a prophet like me from among your own people; you must listen to everything he tells you. [23] Anyone who does not listen to him will be completely cut off from among his people.'

[24] "Indeed, all the prophets from Samuel on, as many as have spoken, have foretold these days. [25] And you are heirs of the prophets and of the covenant God made with your fathers. He said to Abraham, 'Through your offspring all peoples on earth will be blessed.' [26] When God raised up his servant, he sent him first to you to bless you by turning each of you from your wicked ways." (Acts 3:11–26)

After Peter helped to heal a crippled beggar in the name of Jesus, many people on the temple rushed to see them. This set the scene for Peter's second public speech. Peter proclaimed that the healing of the former cripple represented the fulfillment of Old Testament prophecy about the restoration of everything through Jesus. Then, Peter preached repentance and turning to Lord that would result in the forgiveness of sins, times of refreshing from the Lord, and the return of the Lord. Also, the return of the Lord would consummate the messianic age that restores everything.

Peter emphasized the importance of repentance while paraphrasing Moses by implying that the Lord would raise up a messianic prophet and everybody must listen to the Messiah or miss out on the blessings in the messianic age.[1] Evidently, the Old Testament prophecies about the restoration of everything paradoxically never guaranteed that all people would enjoy the blessings of the messianic age. Acts 3:23 indicates that anyone who rejects listening to the Messiah would miss the blessings that God planned to give his people. The blessings of the messianic age are conditioned with the requirements of repentance and turning to the Messiah.

Peter also implied that repentance and turning to the Lord would accelerate times of refreshing and the return of the Lord. This complements (1) the Olivet prophecy in Matthew 24:14 and Mark 13:10 indicating that all nations must hear the gospel before the return of the Lord and 2 Peter 3:11–12 saying that godly living would speed the return of the Lord. Likewise, the return of the Lord is inevitable while human response affects the time frame.

ACTS 7:51–60 AND BLASPHEMY OF THE HOLY SPIRIT

Acts 7:51–60 portrays an interesting response to blasphemy of the Holy Spirit. In these verses, Stephen concludes a speech to the Jewish leaders:

> [51] "You stiff-necked people, with uncircumcised hearts and ears! You are just like your fathers: You always resist the Holy Spirit! [52] Was there ever a prophet your fathers did not persecute? They even killed those who predicted the coming of the Righteous One. And now you have betrayed and murdered him— [53] you who have received the law that was put into effect through angels but have not obeyed it."
>
> [54] When they heard this, they were furious and gnashed their teeth at him. [55] But Stephen, full of the Holy Spirit, looked up to heaven and saw the glory of God, and Jesus standing at the right hand of God. [56] "Look," he said, "I see heaven open and the Son of Man standing at the right hand of God."
>
> [57] At this they covered their ears and, yelling at the top of their voices, they all rushed at him, [58] dragged him out of the city and began to stone him. Meanwhile, the witnesses laid their clothes at the feet of a young man named Saul.
>
> [59] While they were stoning him, Stephen prayed, "Lord Jesus, receive my spirit." [60] Then he fell on his knees and cried out, "Lord, do not hold this sin against them." When he had said this, he fell asleep. (Acts 7:51–60)

---

1. See Deuteronomy 18:15–19.

Stephen was filled with the Holy Spirit and said to the Jewish leaders that he saw heaven open with Jesus standing at the right hand of God. The Jewish leaders covered their ears and yelled at the top of their voices to drown out the sound of Stephen's alleged blasphemous words. They felt indignation while they interpreted Stephen's words as blasphemy that deserved death. They threw stones at Stephen to execute him. Stephen mustered his last words: "Lord, do not hold this sin against them."

These last words of Stephen are amazing. Stephen asked the Lord for the forgiveness of his killers who executed him for alleged blasphemous words that were actually from the Holy Spirit. Also, the "young man named Saul" who oversaw the stoning of Stephen eventually found the forgiveness of the Lord.[2] Additionally, Jesus taught that blasphemy against the Holy Spirit would not be forgiven, while the Gospels according to Matthew and Mark implied that blasphemy against the Holy Spirit related to Jewish leaders declaring that miracles performed by the Spirit were demonic.[3] In the case of Stephen, Jewish leaders accused him of blasphemy because of his words, which actually came from the Holy Spirit. This looks like a clear case of Saul and his minions blaspheming the Holy Spirit, yet Stephen led by the Spirit asked that his killers would find forgiveness. This suggests that Jesus used hyperbole when he said that blasphemy against the Holy Spirit would not be forgiven. That heinous sin has grave consequences while divine forgiveness of that sin is possible.

ACTS 17:29-31

Acts 17:29-31 is an excerpt from a speech that Paul (Saul) delivered to a council in Athens called the Areopagus:

> [29] "Therefore since we are God's offspring, we should not think that the divine being is like gold or silver or stone—an image made by man's design and skill. [30] In the past God overlooked such ignorance, but now he commands all people everywhere to repent. [31] For he has set a day when he will judge the world with justice by the man he has appointed. He has given proof of this to all men by raising him from the dead." (Acts 17:29-31)

---

2. See Acts 9:1-22.
3. See Matthew 12:22-32, Mark 3:22-29, and Luke 12:10.

Paul's speech included the following: (1) all humans are God's offspring; (2) God previously overlooked the ignorance of idolatrous Athenians who made gods out of gold, silver, and stone; (3) God currently commands all people to repent; (4) God will eventually judge the world by an appointed man; (4) God provided evidence of this judgment by raising this appointed man from the dead. One implication of these verses include that the Athenian idolaters who heard the gospel faced a stricter judgment compared to their ancestors who never hear the gospel, which goes along with Luke 12:47–48 teaching that people deserve less punishment for ignorant disobedience compared to knowledgeable disobedience.

12

Letters of Paul and Hebrews

This chapter looks at conditional judgment and the end times in selections from Romans, 1 Corinthians, Philippians, 1 Thessalonians, 2 Thessalonians, and Hebrews.[1]

ROMANS 1:18—5:21

Paul in Romans 1:18—5:21 teaches about the universality of human sin, God's conditional judgment of all humans, and the condition of faith for salvation. All humans except for Jesus Christ have sinned and are subject to God's wrath, but all humans may accept the gift of salvation with abundant grace by accepting faith in Christ. Likewise, conditions are central to both the doctrine of salvation (soteriology) and the doctrine of the end times (eschatology). Also, these verses are foundational to Protestant theology.

1 CORINTHIANS 3:10-15

> [10] By the grace God has given me, I laid a foundation as a wise builder, and someone else is building on it. But each one should build with care. [11] For no one can lay any foundation other than the one already laid, which is Jesus Christ. [12] If anyone builds on this foundation using gold, silver, costly stones, wood, hay or straw, [13] their work will be shown for what it is, because the Day will bring it to light. It will be revealed with fire, and the fire will test the quality of each person's work. [14] If what has been built

---

1. Paul wrote Romans, 1 Corinthians, Philippians, 1 Thessalonians, and 2 Thessalonians in the AD 50s and 60s to churches in the respective cities of Rome (in Italy), Corinth (in Greece), Philippi (in Greece), and Thessalonica (in Greece). An unidentified disciple of Paul wrote Hebrews to churches in various Mediterranean cities.

survives, the builder will receive a reward. ¹⁵ If it is burned up, the builder will suffer loss but yet will be saved—even though only as one escaping through the flames. (1 Corinthians 3:10–15)

Paul in 1 Corinthians 3:10–15 encourages Christians to minister with wisdom and care while he also teaches about judgment day. All ministry needs to be built upon the foundation of Jesus Christ with wisdom and care. Good building material is figuratively referred to as "gold, silver, costly stones" while shoddy building material is referred to "wood, hay or straw." Fire will test all work of the ministry on judgment day. The wood, hay, and straw burn up in the fiery judgment while the gold, silver, and costly stones survive judgment. Likewise, those who built with gold, silver, or costly stones receive reward at judgment day while those who built with wood, hay, or straw suffer loss but still enter heaven. These verses teach about conditions determining rewards for believers at judgment day: obedience and careful ministry results in reward while disobedience and careless ministry results in loss.

1 CORINTHIANS 15:50–58

Paul in 1 Corinthians 15:50–58 teaches about the resurrection and transformation of living believers at the end of human history:

> ⁵⁰ I declare to you, brothers and sisters, that flesh and blood cannot inherit the kingdom of God, nor does the perishable inherit the imperishable. ⁵¹ Listen, I tell you a mystery: We will not all sleep, but we will all be changed— ⁵² in a flash, in the twinkling of an eye, at the last trumpet. For the trumpet will sound, the dead will be raised imperishable, and we will be changed. ⁵³ For the perishable must clothe itself with the imperishable, and the mortal with immortality. ⁵⁴ When the perishable has been clothed with the imperishable, and the mortal with immortality, then the saying that is written will come true: "Death has been swallowed up in victory."
> ⁵⁵ "Where, O death, is your victory? Where, O death, is your sting?"
> ⁵⁶ The sting of death is sin, and the power of sin is the law. ⁵⁷ But thanks be to God! He gives us the victory through our Lord Jesus Christ.
> ⁵⁸ Therefore, my dear brothers and sisters, stand firm. Let nothing move you. Always give yourselves fully to the work of the Lord, because you know that your labor in the Lord is not in vain. (¹ Corinthians 15:50–58)

These verses teach that perishable human flesh will not inherit the everlasting kingdom God. However, the Lord will return and transform all then living believers to imperishable humans and resurrect and transform all dead believers to imperishable humans. The phrase "We will not all sleep" means that all humans will not die before the Lord returns to raise the dead, but there will be a last generation of believers who see the return of the Lord while he quickly transforms them from a perishable body with flesh and blood to an imperishable body, which goes along with Jesus Christ teaching that humans at the resurrection will resemble angels and no longer die.[2] Also, all believers who died will be resurrected and transformed to the same type of imperishable body. Additionally, belief in this end-time transformation takes the sting of death away from believers while encouraging them to live devoutly for the Lord in the present difficult circumstances.

Tension with this teaching about the end-time transformation includes the resurrected Jesus Christ temporarily existing with his perishable human flesh.[3] However, the complete transformation of his human body evidently occurred during the ascension to the Father.[4]

1 THESSALONIANS 4:13-18 AND 5:1-11

This section begins with 1 Thessalonians 4:13-18:

> [13] Brothers and sisters, we do not want you to be uninformed about those who sleep in death, so that you do not grieve like the rest of mankind, who have no hope. [14] For we believe that Jesus died and rose again, and so we believe that God will bring with Jesus those who have fallen asleep in him. [15] According to the Lord's word, we tell you that we who are still alive, who are left until the coming of the Lord, will certainly not precede those who have fallen asleep. [16] For the Lord himself will come down from heaven, with a loud command, with the voice of the archangel and with the trumpet call of God, and the dead in Christ will rise first. [17] After that, we who are still alive and are left will be caught up together with them in the clouds to meet the Lord in the air. And so we will be with the Lord forever. [18] Therefore encourage one another with these words. (1 Thessalonians 4:13-18)

---

2. See Matthew 22:23-33, Mark 12:18-27, and Luke 20:27-40.
3. See Matthew 28:9-10, Luke 24:36-43, and John 20:24-29.
4. See Luke 24:50-52 and Acts 1:9-11.

These verses written by Paul encourage Christians to hope instead of grieve because Jesus rose from the dead and God will resurrect those who died ("fallen asleep") while believing in Jesus. Also, when the Lord returns, those who died in Christ will rise first and then the last generation of believers will be "caught up" and meet the Lord in the air. After this, all believers will enjoy the presence of the Lord forever.

Many Christians use the term *rapture* to designate this event of the last generation of believers being "caught up" to meet with the Lord. This rapture includes each believer's radical transformation from a perishable body to an imperishable body described above in 1 Corinthians 15:50–58.

Paul also says "according to the Lord's word," the resurrection precedes the rapture. However, the words of Jesus Christ in the Gospels and Acts never clearly state this. Jesus taught about a radical transformation at the resurrection where righteous believers resemble angels and never die. Also, as previously mentioned in the Olivet prophecy, Jesus said that during his return angels would gather believers "from the ends of the earth to the ends of the heavens," which plausibly includes the resurrection and the rapture. But none of this clearly indicates that the rapture precedes the resurrection, so perhaps Paul referred to an oral tradition of Jesus unrecorded by the Gospel writers or a direct revelation from Jesus.[5]

The next verses in this section are 1 Thessalonians 5:1–11:

> [1] Now, brothers and sisters, about times and dates we do not need to write to you, [2] for you know very well that the day of the Lord will come like a thief in the night. [3] While people are saying, "Peace and safety," destruction will come on them suddenly, as labor pains on a pregnant woman, and they will not escape.
>
> [4] But you, brothers and sisters, are not in darkness so that this day should surprise you like a thief. [5] You are all children of the light and children of the day. We do not belong to the night or to the darkness. [6] So then, let us not be like others, who are asleep, but let us be awake and sober. [7] For those who sleep, sleep at night, and those who get drunk, get drunk at night. [8] But since we belong to the day, let us be sober, putting on faith and love as a breastplate, and the hope of salvation as a helmet. [9] For God did not appoint us to suffer wrath but to receive salvation through

---

5. John 21:24–25 says that many of the things done by Jesus were never recorded and 2 Corinthians 12:1–10 says that Paul received direct revelation from God.

> our Lord Jesus Christ. ¹⁰ He died for us so that, whether we are awake or asleep, we may live together with him. ¹¹ Therefore encourage one another and build each other up, just as in fact you are doing. (1 Thessalonians 5:1–11)

In 1 Thessalonians 5:1–11, Paul refers to the return of the Lord, the resurrection, and rapture as "the day of the Lord." Also, the day of the Lord includes suffering from destruction.

Verses 5:1–3 focus on the suddenness of the Lord's return for those who face destruction. This includes the imagery of surprise and sudden loss from "a thief in the night" while ironically the people expected "peace and safety." Then, verses 5:4–11 clarify that believers should not face a surprising destruction and suffer wrath from the day of the Lord. Unbelievers face destruction while believers enjoy the rapture described in 4:13–18. Also, Paul uses the imagery of rapture versus destruction to encourage believers to remain spiritually awake and sober.

2 THESSALONIANS 1:6–10 AND 2:1–12

This section begins with 2 Thessalonians 1:6–10:

> ⁶ God is just: He will pay back trouble to those who trouble you ⁷ and give relief to you who are troubled, and to us as well. This will happen when the Lord Jesus is revealed from heaven in blazing fire with his powerful angels. ⁸ He will punish those who do not know God and do not obey the gospel of our Lord Jesus. ⁹ They will be punished with everlasting destruction and shut out from the presence of the Lord and from the glory of his might ¹⁰ on the day he comes to be glorified in his holy people and to be marveled at among all those who have believed. This includes you, because you believed our testimony to you. (2 Thessalonians 1:6–10)

Paul in 2 Thessalonians 1:6–10 pronounces that the glorious return of the Lord will bring relief to believers by destroying perpetrators of ungodly persecution, and believers will marvel at the presence of the returning Lord. However, I side with Thomas Talbott and hold that various modern English translations including the New International Version mistranslate the biblical Greek preposition *apo* in 2 Thessalonians 1:9.[6] The Greek *apo* commonly translates to "from" while depending on the context *apo* could mean "comes from" or "away from." In the case of

---

6. See Talbott, "A Pauline Interpretation of Divine Judgment."

the above translation, *apo* is translated to the phrase *and shut out from*. For example, without the added phrase, verse 1:9 would read, "They will be punished with everlasting destruction from the presence of the Lord and from the glory of his might." Given no other information, this could mean that the everlasting destruction makes people go "away from" the Lord as in "shut out from" or that the everlasting destruction "comes from" the Lord. Moreover, the latter is most consistent with Paul's theme of destruction from the presence of the Lord in the two letters to the Thessalonians, which is evident in 1 Thessalonians 5:3 and 2 Thessalonians 2:8.

As discussed earlier, 1 Thessalonians 5:3 describes sudden destruction coming from the return of the Lord. Also, 2 Thessalonians 2:8 pronounces the destruction of the man of lawlessness coming from the return of the Lord. Given this context, the translation of 2 Thessalonians 1:9 apparently should read, "They will be punished with everlasting destruction coming from the presence of the Lord and from the glory of his might."

The next verses in this section are 2 Thessalonians 2:1-12:

> [1] Concerning the coming of our Lord Jesus Christ and our being gathered to him, we ask you, brothers and sisters, [2] not to become easily unsettled or alarmed by the teaching allegedly from us—whether by a prophecy or by word of mouth or by letter—asserting that the day of the Lord has already come. [3] Don't let anyone deceive you in any way, for that day will not come until the rebellion occurs and the man of lawlessness is revealed, the man doomed to destruction. [4] He will oppose and will exalt himself over everything that is called God or is worshiped, so that he sets himself up in God's temple, proclaiming himself to be God.
>
> [5] Don't you remember that when I was with you I used to tell you these things? [6] And now you know what is holding him back, so that he may be revealed at the proper time. [7] For the secret power of lawlessness is already at work; but the one who now holds it back will continue to do so till he is taken out of the way. [8] And then the lawless one will be revealed, whom the Lord Jesus will overthrow with the breath of his mouth and destroy by the splendor of his coming. [9] The coming of the lawless one will be in accordance with how Satan works. He will use all sorts of displays of power through signs and wonders that serve the lie, [10] and all the ways that wickedness deceives those who are perishing. They perish because they refused to love the truth and so be saved.

> [11] For this reason God sends them a powerful delusion so that they will believe the lie [12] and so that all will be condemned who have not believed the truth but have delighted in wickedness. (2 Thessalonians 2:1–12)

Paul in 2 Thessalonians 2:1–12 prophesied about the return of the Lord and preceding events. Some people in the Thessalonian church evidently alarmed believers by saying that the Lord had already returned. Paul responded to this by proclaiming that "the rebellion" and revelation of "the man of lawlessness" must occur before the return of the Lord.

Verses 2:1–2 say that the coming of the Lord and our being gathered to him had not already occurred, despite the proclamation of some so-called prophecies. The "being gathered to him" refers to the rapture described in 1 Thessalonians 4:13—5:11, while "the day of Lord" includes both the coming of the Lord and the rapture. Then, the next verses proclaim what must occur before the day of the Lord.

Paul in 2 Thessalonians 2:3–4 proclaims that the "rebellion" and the revelation of the "man of lawlessness" must occur before the day of the Lord. The "rebellion" in verse 2:3 translates from the Greek word *apostasia*, which commonly translates to the word *apostasy*. Apostasy refers to rebellion. In this case, the rebellion analogizes "the rebellion that causes desolation" in Daniel 8:13 and 8:23–25, which as discussed in chapter 9 was initially the atrocities and destruction of Antiochus. Also, verse 2:4 describes the man of lawlessness by using language that alludes to Daniel 11:36–37. Likewise, the "rebellion" in 2 Thessalonians 2:3 refers to the future rebellion of the man of lawlessness that ends in his destruction.

Verses 2:5–12 indicate that God holds back the man of lawlessness until God's timing, while the power of lawlessness is already working to some degree. Also, the revelation of the man of lawlessness will be a satanic work that includes powerful signs and wonders that deceive people who delight in wickedness. Moreover, the return of the Lord will overthrow the man of lawlessness.

The man of lawlessness is a clear picture of the end-time evil person with great power called *the antichrist*. Paul said that the power of the antichrist was already at work while the antichrist and his rebellion would be revealed before the rapture and return of the Lord. Regardless of this apparent chronology, many hold to the doctrine of the pretribulation rapture.[7]

The doctrine of pretribulationism says that the rapture occurs before the great tribulation caused by the final antichrist, while the doctrine focuses on the sudden and unpredictable timing of the rapture. The doctrine deduces that since AD 70 there is no sign such as the appearance and rebellion of the antichrist that must precede the rapture, or else the timing of the rapture would be predictable. The doctrine also specifies that the rapture is a secret that precedes the glorious cosmic epiphany when the Lord returns to earth.[8] However, the scenario above by Paul indicates that the rebellion of the antichrist occurs before the day of the Lord, which includes the rapture. Additionally, the day of the Lord destroys the antichrist. This places the rapture simultaneous to the end of the tribulation, which is called the *post-tribulation rapture*.[9]

In regards to conditional futurism, according to the teaching of Hebrew prophets outlined in chapter 1, the antichrist could read this prophecy about his destruction and genuinely repent in the name of the Lord Jesus Christ. Likewise, the antichrist could avoid this doom.

PHILIPPIANS 2:5–11

Philippians 2:5–11 encourages believers to follow the humble example of Jesus Christ while these verses also teach about the end-time fulfillment of Isaiah 45:22–24 declaring that everybody will turn and bow to the Lord (YHWH). Philippians 2:6–8 teaches that Christ is both the nature of God and the nature of a human servant who obeyed to the point of dying on a cross, while verses 2:9–11 say:

> [9] Therefore God exalted him to the highest place
> and gave him the name that is above every name,
> [10] that at the name of Jesus every knee should bow,
> in heaven and on earth and under the earth,
> [11] and every tongue acknowledge that Jesus Christ is Lord,
> to the glory of God the Father. (Philippians 2:9–11)

---

7. See Walvoord, *The Rapture Question*.

8. The time frame for pretribulationism is that the rapture precedes the rest of the return of the Lord by seven years based on interpretations from Daniel (Walvoord, 11–20).

9. See Ladd, *The Blessed Hope*.

These verses partially parallel the Lord in Isaiah 45:22–24 declaring that there is no other God and that "Before me every knee will bow, by me every tongue will swear." Every knee bowing to Jesus and every tongue confessing that he is Lord according to Philippians 2:9–11 will fulfill the end-time prophecy in Isaiah.

HEBREWS 6:4–8 AND 10:26–31

> [4] It is impossible for those who have once been enlightened, who have tasted the heavenly gift, who have shared in the Holy Spirit, [5] who have tasted the goodness of the word of God and the powers of the coming age [6] and who have fallen away, to be brought back to repentance. To their loss they are crucifying the Son of God all over again and subjecting him to public disgrace. [7] Land that drinks in the rain often falling on it and that produces a crop useful to those for whom it is farmed receives the blessing of God. [8] But land that produces thorns and thistles is worthless and is in danger of being cursed. In the end it will be burned. (Hebrews 6:4–8)

A literal interpretation of Hebrews 6:4–8 indicates that genuine believers who have fallen away from their faith in God are beyond restoration. However, this appears to conflict with the Old Testament prophets calling the wicked Israelites to repentance and restoration. Likewise, verses 6:4–8 could have been a powerful warning to believers against giving up their faith while using hyperbole in the tradition of the Lord Jesus Christ, which would be consistent with the biblical theme of God calling his wicked people to repentance. Also, the Reformed tradition says that no genuine believer could ever abandon their salvation, which necessitates an interpretation that these verses powerfully and *figuratively* warn against abandoning faith. Conversely, conditional futurism says the figurativeness applies to the impossibility of restoration. Another related verse is Hebrews 10:26–31, which warns that deliberate sin after receiving knowledge of the gospel results in fearful judgment.

13

Letters of Peter, John, and Jude

THIS CHAPTER LOOKS AT the ancient controversy of Christ's proclamation according to 1 Peter 3:19-20 and 4:6, the judgment of false teachers in 2 Peter 2, the return of the Lord in 2 Peter 3:1-13, the final antichrist and other antichrists in the letters of John, and the judgment of godless people in Jude.

1 PETER 3:18—4:6

This section focuses on 3:19-20 and 4:6 while looking at the context of 1 Peter 3:18—4:6:

> [18] For Christ also suffered once for sins, the righteous for the unrighteous, to bring you to God. He was put to death in the body but made alive in the Spirit. [19] After being made alive, he went and made proclamation to the imprisoned spirits— [20] to those who were disobedient long ago when God waited patiently in the days of Noah while the ark was being built. In it only a few people, eight in all, were saved through water, [21] and this water symbolizes baptism that now saves you also—not the removal of dirt from the body but the pledge of a clear conscience toward God. It saves you by the resurrection of Jesus Christ, [22] who has gone into heaven and is at God's right hand—with angels, authorities and powers in submission to him.
>
> [1] Therefore, since Christ suffered in his body, arm yourselves also with the same attitude, because whoever suffers in the body is done with sin. [2] As a result, they do not live the rest of their earthly lives for evil human desires, but rather for the will of God. [3] For you have spent enough time in the past doing what pagans choose to do—living in debauchery, lust, drunkenness, orgies, carousing and detestable idolatry. [4] They are surprised that you

do not join them in their reckless, wild living, and they heap abuse on you. ⁵ But they will have to give account to him who is ready to judge the living and the dead. ⁶ For this is the reason the gospel was preached even to those who are now dead, so that they might be judged according to human standards in regard to the body, but live according to God in regard to the spirit. (1 Peter 3:18—4:6)

The above verses 3:18—4:6 primarily teach about the suffering of believers and the example of Christ's suffering. However, controversy surrounds verses 3:19–20 and 4:6. Verses 3:19–20 say that Christ made proclamation to "imprisoned spirits" who disobeyed long ago in the days of Noah, while verse 3:18 indicates that this proclamation occurred after the earthly death of Christ. Also, verse 4:6 says that the gospel was preached to those who are now dead, while this gospel could result in the hearers both facing judgment and living according to God.

These verses became a basis for what the ancient church called *the descent of Christ into hell* or *the harrowing of hell,* which is a prominent doctrine in the Roman Catholic Church and Orthodox Church.[1] Early references to the descent of Christ include Irenaeus in the second century AD. Irenaeus referred to 1 Peter while saying that Christ descended into the regions beneath the earth and preached to the departed Old Testament righteous believers.[2] Also, Clement of Alexandria in the second to third centuries AD referred to 1 Peter while saying that Christ died and preached to the Jews and Gentiles (non-Jews) in Hades, the abode of the dead, while Clement specifically argued against those such as Irenaeus who said that Christ descended into Hades and preached only to the Old Testament righteous.[3] Clement's controversial interpretation indicates postmortem conversions to Christ, which is the postmortem Christian conversion of people who died as unbelievers.

These competing interpretations of 1 Peter 3:19–20 and 4:6 persisted in the ancient church. For example, Origen was a third century AD student of Clement, and Origen said 1 Peter indicated that the disobedient people who died in Noah's flood had postmortem hope of

---

1. See Aquinas, *Third Part of Summa Theologica,* Question 52 and Alfeyev, "Christ the Conqueror of Hell."
2. See Irenaeus, *Against Heresies,* Book 4, chapter 27, paragraph 2.
3. See Clement of Alexandria, *The Stromata,* Book 6, chapter 6.

salvation.[4] Also, Gregory of Nyssa in the fourth century AD delivered a sermon on the three days between the death and resurrection of Christ while implicitly referring to 1 Peter 3:19–20 and 4:6 and explicitly teaching about the postmortem conversions of millions of souls spanning every generations before the death of Christ.[5] Additionally, Origen and Gregory taught about the hope of God eventually restoring all departed people to salvation, which they called the *apocatastasis* (restoration).[6]

Another important slice of ancient church history related to the descent of Christ into hell involves AD 414 letters between Bishop Evodius and Bishop Augustine.[7] Evodius asked Augustine:

> Who are those spirits in reference to whom the apostle Peter testifies concerning the Lord in these words: "Being put to death in the flesh, but quickened in the spirit, in which also He went and preached to the spirits in prison?" giving us to understand that they were in hell, and that Christ descending into hell, preached the gospel to them all, and by grace delivered them all from darkness and punishment, so that from the time of the resurrection of the Lord judgment is expected, hell having then been completely emptied.[8]

Evodius asked Augustine about the identity of the "imprisoned spirits" in 1 Peter 3:19. Evodius also indicated a widespread belief in the early fifth century church that 1 Peter taught about Christ descending into hell, preaching to all people in hell, and emptying hell.

Augustine replied with a long letter while expressing his uncertainty about the identity of the imprisoned spirits.[9] He also reflected on four views that were common in the early fifth century church:

1. Some Christians taught that Christ preached in hell only to the righteous Jews.

2. Some Christians taught that Christ preached in hell to everybody but preaching in hell stopped after the resurrection of Christ.

---

4. See Origin, *De Principiis*, Book 2, "On Justice and Goodness."
5. See Gregory of Nyssa, "On the Three Day Period," 36–38.
6. See Blowers, "Apokatastasis," 36–37.
7. See Augustine, *Letters of St. Augustin,* Letters 163 and 164. Evodius wrote to Augustine in Letter 163 while Augustine replied to Evodius in Letter 164.
8. Evodius in Augustine, *Letters of St. Augustin,* Letter 163.
9. Augustine, *Letters of St. Augustin,* Letter 164.

3. Some Christians taught that Christ preached in hell to everybody and preaching in hell to those who never heard the gospel continued.
4. Some Christians taught that Christ preached in hell to everybody and preaching in hell to everybody continued.

Augustine disagreed with all of these views. For example, he disagreed with the first view, which is along the lines of Irenaeus's view and is similar to the most common Roman Catholic and Orthodox view. Augustine argued that righteous Jews such as Abraham and Lazarus were in paradise, so Christ could not have preached to them in hell if they were in paradise. Augustine also argued that Christ preached to nobody in hell and innovated the interpretation that 1 Peter 4:6 taught about Christ preaching to the *spiritually* dead.

Augustine also around AD 413–426 in *The City of God* strongly disagreed with Christians who taught that no human would be punished literally forever, but he saw this doctrine of postmortem conversion starting with Christ's descent into hell as an "amicable controversy." For example, Augustine referred to a church condemnation of Origen's followers who taught about postmortem conversions and worst of all that saints would forever alternate between periods of misery and happiness, but Augustine considered many others who believed in postmortem conversion were wrong but within the orthodox community of Christian faith.[10]

As noted above, Augustine referred to a church condemnation of various teachings associated with Origen, who as earlier mentioned was from the third century AD. A similar condemnation was formalized in the AD 553 Fifth Ecumenical Council, which declared fifteen points of condemnation against doctrines associated with Origen. Emperor Justinian convened the council while one of his goals was to officially condemn Origin's teaching about the eventual restoration of all wicked humans and angels in hell, the apocatastasis. Ironically, Justinian in his letter recited during the first session of the council declared that the council should hold fast to the previous four ecumenical councils and various holy fathers including Gregory of Nyssa.[11] Evidently, the Fifth

---

10. Augustine, *The City of God*, Book 21: "Of the Eternal Punishment," chapter 17: "Of Those Who Fancy that No Men Shall Be Punished Eternally."

11. See Percival, *The Seven Ecumenical Councils*, "The Fifth Ecumenical Council."

Ecumenical Council condemned the apocatastasis of Origin while honoring Gregory and his teachings that included another version of the restoration of wicked people in hell. Regardless, teachings about postmortem conversions waned in the church after the council's official condemnation of Origen's doctrines while Augustine's interpretation of hell dominated the western church led by Rome.

The evidence in ancient church history including Augustine's writings indicates that belief in Christ preaching in hell was a widespread orthodox option in the ancient church. However, various opponents of that doctrine misinterpret church history. For example, Charles Hodge in 1871 incorrectly claimed that the universal church rejects that Christ preached the gospel in hell,[12] unless Hodge talked about his contemporary universal church while disregarding the history of the universal church. Also, twentieth- and twenty-first-century proponents of the belief that Christ preached the gospel in hell include Roman Catholic theologian Hans Urs von Balthasar, Reformed theologian Jurgen Moltmann, and Russian Orthodox bishop Hilarion Alfeyev.[13]

Conditional futurism works with or without the orthodox option of belief in Christ preaching the gospel to the wicked dead according to 1 Peter. In the case that Christ preached the gospel to the wicked dead, then conditions applied to the gospel for the dead. For example, the wicked dead could accept or reject the gospel. Also, 1 Peter 4:6 describes judgment in regard to the body, which indicates inescapable judgment regardless of the duration of the punishment.

Additionally, any discussion of Christ preaching the gospel to the dead must address the question that Evodius asked Augustine: Who are those "imprisoned spirits" according to Peter?[14] The question is controversial because the imagery of the imprisoned spirits refers to the fallen angels who married human women and propagated hybrid giants called *the Nephilim* according to the apocalyptic book of Watchers in 1 Enoch,[15] which elaborated on Genesis 6:1–8. A major part of the controversy involves the plausibility of male angels and female humans propagat-

---

12. Hodge, *Systematic Theology: II*, 618–621.
13. See Balthasar, *Mysterium Paschale*, 148–188; Moltmann "Descent into Hell"; and Alfeyev, "Christ the Conqueror of Hell."
14. Evodius in Augustine, *Letters of St. Augustin*, Letter 163.
15. The book of Watchers is 1 Enoch 1–36, while 1 Enoch has 108 chapters.

ing hybrid giants. For example, Irenaeus accepted the plausibility and Augustine rejected the plausibility.[16]

I propose a supposedly new model for these fallen angels and the Nephilim that goes along with my comment in chapter 3. The Nephilim were not biological hybrids but humans because their fathers were angelophanies with human bodies.[17] This proposal begins by analyzing Genesis 6:1–8:

> [1] When human beings began to increase in number on the earth and daughters were born to them, [2] the sons of God saw that the daughters of humans were beautiful, and they married any of them they chose. [3] Then the LORD said, "My Spirit will not contend with humans forever, for they are mortal; their days will be a hundred and twenty years."
>
> [4] The Nephilim were on the earth in those days—and also afterward—when the sons of God went to the daughters of humans and had children by them. They were the heroes of old, men of renown.
>
> [5] The LORD saw how great man's wickedness on the earth had become, and that every inclination of the thoughts of his heart was only evil all the time. [6] The LORD was grieved that he had made man on the earth, and his heart was filled with pain. [7] So the LORD said, "I will wipe mankind, whom I have created, from the face of the earth—men and animals, and creatures that move along the ground, and birds of the air—for I am grieved that I have made them." [8] But Noah found favor in the eyes of the LORD. (Genesis 6:1–8)

Genesis 6:2 says that the sons of God developed sexual attraction for various human daughters while marrying any of them that they chose, which evidently included polygyny. Then, verse 6:3 says that God planned judgment for the humans. Next, verse 6:4 says that the sons of God and human daughters propagated heroic Nephilim, who lived then and afterwards. The following verses, Genesis 6:5–8, say that the wicked-

---

16. See Irenaeus, *Against Heresies,* Book 4, chapter 36, paragraph 4; and Augustine, *The City of God,* Book 15: "The Progress of the Earthly and Heavenly Cities," chapter 23: "Whether We are to Believe that Angels."

17. I introduced this model of fallen angels and the Nephilim in "Orthodoxy and Gregory of Nyssa's Universalism," *TheoPerspectives* (blog), October 31, 2007, http://theoperspectives.blogspot.com/2007/10/orthodoxy-and-gregory-of-nyssas.html.

ness of humanity increased while the Lord planned to punish humanity with extinction apart from Noah and his family.

The book of Watchers in 1 Enoch imaginatively elaborated on Genesis 6:1–8 with an apocalypse. The apocalypse says that a group of heavenly angels called the *watchers* decided to abandon their charge as guardians of humanity while they lusted for beautiful human women and took an oath that they would each marry a woman. The fallen angels and their human wives propagated hybrid giants—that is, the Nephilim. The fallen angels taught humans about various secrets such as metal weaponry and enchantments. The hybrid giants stole all the food from the humans and eventually began to eat the humans. The Lord pronounced judgment against the humans and giants because of their wickedness: the Lord sent the holy angel Uriel to warn Noah about the flood that would destroy everything on the earth; the Lord sent the holy angel Raphael to bind Aseal, a leader of the fallen angels, and cast him into darkness with sharp jagged stones beneath him while Aseal would see nothing but darkness until judgment day when he is led to the fiery punishment; the Lord told the holy angel Gabriel to oppose the giant children of the fallen angels and instigate them to fight among themselves to destroy each other; the Lord told the holy angel Michael to bind the other fallen angels who would see the death of their giant children and suffer bondage for seventy generations until judgment day when they are thrown into the prison of the fiery abyss forever. The fallen watchers asked the Lord to forgive both themselves and their hybrid children, but the Lord forever rejected their request. Also, when the hybrid giants died, they became the demon spirits who roam the earth and antagonize humans.

Many interpreters reject that Christ preached the gospel to imprisoned spirits while agreeing that (1) the "sons of God" in Genesis 6:1–4 refers to fallen angels and (2) 1 Peter 3:19–20 refers to the imprisonment of those fallen angels.[18] My model explains how angels with human bodies fell and propagated children with human women. For example, Genesis 18:1—19:25 teaches about angels appearing as humans. The verses begin with the Lord appearing to Abraham while Abraham sees three men. These men are three angels visiting Abraham. The angels with human bodies conversed, ate, and drank with Abraham. Later, the men from Sodom wanted to sexually rape two of the angelic men. These details indicate that the angels had a digestive tract and sex appeal

---

18. See Ericson, "Spirits in Prison."

while suggesting that these angels appeared in human bodies, which I call *human angelophanies*. Also, Hebrews 13:2 says that some people showed hospitality to angels while thinking that the angels were human. In the light of these apparent human angelophanies, I propose that Genesis 6:1–4 teaches that some human angelophanies disregarded their charge to guard humans and married any of the beautiful women that they chose.

The Bible describes human angelophanies while never discussing the origins of the respective human bodies. Perhaps the biblical focus of angels suddenly appearing suggests that their adult human bodies suddenly formed, which I call *fiat human angelophanies*. Alternatively, perhaps the biological bodies of the human angelophanies formed normally in human wombs, which I call *incarnate human angelophanies*. In either case, a human angelophany might be a "hypostatic union" of a preexistent angelic nature and newly formed human nature comparable to the hypostatic union of the divine nature and human nature of the Lord Jesus Christ as defined in the AD 451 Fourth Ecumenical Council.[19]

Advantages of interpreting that the sons of God who propagated heroic progeny were human angelophanies include that the interpretation is consistent with ancient and modern understanding of mammalian reproduction. For example, ancient Mediterranean farmers understood that the parents of mammalian hybrids had comparable anatomy and the mammalian hybrids were mostly infertile, while two mammal species with drastic anatomical differences could never crossbreed. Also, modern science indicates that parents of mammalian hybrids have comparable chromosomes, but the differences in the chromosomes typically hinder the fertility of the hybrids. However, Numbers 13:31–33 says that the sons of Anak descended from evidently fertile Nephilim, so the angelic ancestor of Anak likely had human (*Homo sapiens*) chromosomes instead of nearly human chromosomes. Moreover, this interpretation avoids a literal interpretation of 1 Enoch that (1) was an apocalypse and (2) never achieved canonicity in most Jewish and Christian communities.[20] For instance, the apocalyptic authors of 1 Enoch might never have intended to teach about literal hybrid giants who died and became

---

19. See Percival, *The Seven Ecumenical Councils*, "The Fourth Ecumenical Council."

20. Among Jewish and Christian communities, only the Ethiopian Beta Israel (Jews of Ethiopia) and the Ethiopian Orthodox Church include 1 Enoch in their canon of Scripture.

demons any more than John the Revelator intended to teach about an appearance of a literal beast with seven heads and ten horns. Likewise, Peter's reference to the imagery in 1 Enoch never affirmed the historicity or canonicity of 1 Enoch.[21] Another advantage of interpreting that Genesis 6:1-4 refers to human angelophanies is that the judgment in the rest of Genesis 6 focuses on the wickedness of humanity, which in this interpretation includes the wickedness of human angelophanies and their heroic human progeny.

This interpretation of 1 Peter 3:19-20 and 4:6 says that Jesus Christ died and descended into the abode of the dead while preaching the gospel to all the dead, including the worst class of wicked humanity who were the fallen human angelophanies. Their human bodies had died while they ended up as imprisoned spirits. The dead who heard the gospel could accept or reject the gospel. Those who accepted the gospel faced judgment in regards to their sins while living with an earthly body, but they would eventually enjoy redemption. This flipped 1 Enoch 14, which said that the fallen angels asked the Lord to forgive them and their heroic children while the Lord forever rejected their request. Then, Christ after his resurrection and before his ascension taught Peter and the other apostles about the kingdom of God,[22] which included Christ telling them about the events in 1 Peter 3:19-20 and 4:6. Next, Christ ascended back to active heavenly rule alongside the Father while all spiritual forces and authorities of evil in the heavenly realms submitted to him.[23] Additionally, conditional futurism works with or without this particular interpretation of Christ's death.

2 PETER 2

Second Peter 2 warns about false teachers who introduce destructive heresies such as denying the Lord while these false teachers face horrific judgment. For example, 2 Peter 2:4 refers to the judgment of the fallen angels in 1 Enoch who suffered in Tartarus with "chains of darkness" while waiting for judgment, and 2 Peter 2:17 says that "blackest dark-

---

21. Jesus told Peter about the events between his death and resurrection while Silas assisted Peter with writing 1 Peter, so the choice of language that described the events could have originated with Jesus, Peter, or Silas.

22. See Acts 1:3.

23. See the Ephesians 6:12 reference to evil "authorities" and "spiritual forces of evil in the heavenly realms."

ness is reserved" for the false teachers. Also, verses 2:20–22 warns that anybody who found freedom from corruption by knowing the Lord and then turns away from the Lord by following destructive heresies ends up worse off than if he never knew the Lord in the first place.

2 PETER 3:1–13

Second Peter 3:1–13 continues by describing the return of the Lord. Before the Lord returns, scoffers will ridicule by claiming that the Lord has not returned as he promised. But as mentioned in chapter 10, 2 Peter 3:8–9 says that the Lord's timing is completely different than human timing; for example, in the perspective of the Lord, a day is like a thousand years while a thousand years are like a day. So the Lord is not slow in keeping his promise while the Lord wants nobody to perish. However, the Lord will return and use fire for the destruction of the heavens, earth, and ungodly people while providing a new heaven and a new earth for righteous people. Also, verse 3:11 encourage believers to live godly lives, which is a condition for living in the new heaven and new earth.

LETTERS OF JOHN ON ANTICHRIST AND ANTICHRISTS

> Dear children, this is the last hour; and as you have heard that the antichrist is coming, even now many antichrists have come. This is how we know it is the last hour. (1 John 2:18)

First John 2:18 indicates that the original audience of the respective letter had expected the appearance of the final antichrist. The reference to the antichrist included no introduction or definition because the audience already knew about the antichrist, evidently from teachings such as 2 Thessalonians 2.[24] However, 1 John 2:18 also says that many antichrists had already come while verse 2:22 says that anybody who denies that Jesus is the Christ is an antichrist. These verses teach about many prefigurations of the final antichrist who are false teachers. This is similar to 1 John 4:3, which says that in one context the spirit of the antichrist is coming in the future while in another context the spirit of the antichrist is already in false teachers who teach that Jesus is not from God. Also, 2 John 1:7 says that any teacher who teaches that Jesus did not come in

---

24. See chapter 12.

flesh is the deceiver and the antichrist, which associates the false teachers with both the devil (the deceiver) and the antichrist.

JUDE

The letter of Jude is a powerful chapter that warns ungodly teachers and their followers in a way that is comparable to 2 Peter 2. Jude warns that so-called believers who live ungodly lives and deny that Jesus is the Christ will face horrific judgment, while Jude makes two references to judgment in 1 Enoch. For example, Jude 1:6 compares the judgment of the ungodly to the 1 Enoch accounts of angels who abandoned their authority and consequently suffered bondage from chains in darkness until judgment day. Also, Jude 1:14–15 refers to 1 Enoch 1:9 while saying that the person Enoch prophesied that the Lord would come with thousands upon thousands of his holy ones to punish the ungodly and convict them of their ungodliness.

14

The Eighth King in Revelation

THE APOCALYPSE IN THE book of Revelation primarily reveals Jesus Christ, while the apocalypse also reveals the horrifically powerful king and kingdom called *the beast*. Revelation 17 interprets the complexity of this beast. Verse 17:3 describes a scarlet red beast covered with blasphemous names while the beast has seven heads and ten horns. Also, verse 17:8 says that the beast previously appeared, then ceased to exist, and eventually reappeared while going to its destruction. Next, verses 17:9–14 interpret symbolism in this portrait of the beast:

1. The seven heads of the beast represent the Seven Hills of Rome.
2. The seven heads of the beast also represent a political lineage of kings/emperors.
3. In the context of the original audience of Revelation, five of the kings previously existed, one currently exists, and one is yet to come.
4. The beast also represents an eighth king who comes from the seven.
5. That final king appears, then ceases to exist, and reappears while going to his destruction.
6. The ten horns of the beast represent ten kings who support the final king while he rules over them.

Other symbolism in these verses include the biblical numbers *seven*, *eight*, and *ten*. Seven and ten represent completeness while eight represents resurrection and new beginning.[1] This case involves the complete-

---

1. Bullinger, *Number in Scripture*, 150–151 for "seven," 181 for "eight," and 227 for "ten."

ness and resurrection of evil. Also, the reappearance of the beast refers to the Nero redivivus legend that said the former Roman emperor Nero would return after his AD 68 death, which evidently places the writing of Revelation after the origin of the redivivus legend. Additionally, Revelation 14–18 uses the word *Babylon* on six occasions while referring to the government of the beast, which also identifies the eighth king with Babylonian king Nebuchadnezzar.[2]

Some futurist scholars look at 1 John referring to many antichrists and the kingdom aspect of the beast in the symbolic apocalyptic literature while questioning if the eighth king is an evil individual human or instead an evil governmental force without a primary human leader.[3] In other words, the final antichrist is not an individual human who leads a government but a governmental force without a primary a human leader. I feel sympathy for this view and see no grounds for rigid dogmatisms about various details in Revelation because of the apocalyptic nature of the literature, but I also suppose that the prophecy of the man of lawlessness in 2 Thessalonians supports that the eighth king is an individual human while Revelation 17:9–14 suggests that the beast is both a king and a kingdom. Conditional futurism could work with various views of the antichrist while I propose that the final antichrist is a primary human leader of a government.

Revelation 11–21 prophesied the apocalyptic account of the beast. The next sections of this chapter recount and interpret this prophecy.

THE BEAST IN REVELATION 11

In Revelation 11:1–6, an angel says that the Gentiles will trample the holy city for forty-two months while two powerful Christian witnesses prophesy for 1,260 days, which is also forty-two months. If any enemy tries to harm the two witnesses, then fire comes from their mouths and destroys the enemy. The two witnesses could also prevent rain while they prophesy, turn waters into blood, and strike the earth with every kind of plague.

In Revelation 11:7, after the two witnesses complete their prophecy, "the beast that comes up from the Abyss will attack them, and overpower them and kill them."

---

2. See Nebuchadnezzar in chapters 1, 6, and 9.
3. Bauckham and Hart, *Hope against Hope*, 110–116.

In Revelation 11:8–10, the dead bodies of the two witnesses lie in public view for three and half days while all the world gazes at their bodies and refuses them burial. The world celebrates the death of the prophets who tormented the people of the world. But after three and half days, God resurrects the two witnesses while terror struck all who saw the resurrection. Then, a voice from heaven called the two witnesses up and they ascended to a cloud while their enemies watched. Next, a severe earthquake collapsed a tenth of the city while seven thousand people died. The survivors felt terror and gave glory to God.

Revelation 11:11–19 showed angelic beings praising God while declaring God's reign on earth and the destruction of God's enemies.

Points of interpretation include the following. The forty-two months of gentiles trampling the holy city analogizes the abomination that causes desolation in Daniel and the Olivet prophecy, which related to the 168 BC overthrow of Jerusalem and the AD 70 destruction of Jerusalem.[4] The two powerful Christian witnesses symbolize the great lawgiver and prophet Moses and the great prophet Elijah who appeared in the Transfiguration while the two witnesses also symbolize the power of the church. Without introduction, the apocalypse says that the beast comes up from the Abyss and kills the two powerful Christian witnesses. The beast appearing from the Abyss signifies the demonic nature of the beast while the connection with the forty-two months of trampling the holy city analogizes the beast with the abomination that causes desolation, Seleucid king Antiochus IV Epiphanes, and the Roman general Titus who became Emperor Titus. The beast also analogizes the various evil beasts in Daniel.

THE DRAGON IN REVELATION 12

Revelation 12:1–6 jumps to a scene with two great signs. The first sign is a woman clothed with the sun, the moon under her feet, and a crown of twelve stars on her head. She was pregnant and cried out while suffering labor pains. The second sign is the devil appearing as an enormous red dragon with seven heads, seven crowns, and ten horns. The dragon's tale swept a third of the stars from the sky and stood in front of the pregnant woman while waiting to devour her child at the moment of birth. She gave birth to a son who will rule all the nations with an iron scepter.

---

4. See chapters 9 and 10.

God took the child to his throne while the woman fled into a divinely protected wilderness for 1,260 days.

Revelation 12:7–17 describes a war in the heavenly realms. The archangel Michael and his angels opposed the dragon and his angels. The dragon and his angels lost their place in heaven while thrown to the earth. Then, the enraged dragon waged war against the rest of the woman's children.

Points of interpretation include that the woman giving birth and her children represent believers while the third of stars swept from the sky represents fallen angels, which refers to rebellious stars in 1 Enoch 17–19.

THE BEAST IN REVELATION 13

Revelation 13:1–4 reintroduces the beast. The dragon stood at the shore of the sea while a beast came out of the sea. The beast similar to the dragon had seven heads and ten horns, but the beast had ten crowns compared to dragon's seven crowns. Each of the ten crowns had a blasphemous name. The beast resembled a leopard but with feet like a bear and a mouth like a lion. The dragon gave the beast his power, governmental throne, and authority. One of the heads of the beast appeared fatally wounded, but the fatal wound healed while the entire world filled with wonder and followed the beast. People worshiped the dragon and the beast while saying that nobody could wage war against the beast.

Revelation 13:5–10 says that the beast reigned for forty-two months. He slandered God and waged war against the people of God while conquering them. The beast ruled all of the nations. Everybody on earth worshiped the beast except for believers in Christ.

Revelation 13:11–18 introduces a second beast. This beast came out of the earth and had two horns like a lamb but spoke like a dragon. He exercised all of the authority of the first beast while performing signs such as making fire come down from the sky. He made an idol in the image of the first beast and made everybody on earth worship the first beast and the idol or else face death. The second beast also managed the infamous mark of the beast—that is, 666, which citizens needed for any commercial trade.

Points of interpretation include the following:

1. The reintroduction of the beast indicates that Revelation focuses on themes instead of chronology.
2. The beast coming from the sea analogizes the kings represented as beasts coming out of the sea in Daniel 7.
3. The beast coming from the sea also symbolizes the leviathan sea monster imagery in Psalm 74:14 and Isaiah 27:1.
4. The beast recovering from the fatal wound refers to the Nero redivivus legend.
5. The carnage of the second beast killing everybody who refuses to worship the first beast and his idol described the great tribulation according to Revelation 7:9–17, which pictures a multitude of saints martyred in the "great tribulation" who afterwards wore white robes while surrounding God's heavenly throne.

THE BEAST IN REVELATION 14

Revelation 14:6–13 describes three angels making proclamations that will be heard by all people on earth.

The first angel in verse 14:7 proclaimed:

> Hear God and give him glory, because the hour of his judgment has come. Worship him who made the heavens, the earth, the sea and the springs of water. (Revelation 14:7)

The second angel in verse 14:8 proclaimed:

> 'Fallen! Fallen is Babylon the Great,' which made all the nations drink the maddening wine of her adulteries. (Revelation 14:8)

The third angel in verses 14:9–11 proclaimed:

> If anyone worships the beast and its image and receives its mark on their forehead or on their hand, [10] they, too, will drink the wine of God's fury, which has been poured full strength into the cup of his wrath. They will be tormented with burning sulfur in the presence of the holy angels and of the Lamb. [11] And the smoke of their torment will rise for ever and ever. There will be no rest day or night for those who worship the beast and its image, or for anyone who receives the mark of its name. (Revelation 14:9–11)

Points of interpretation include that a proclamation to worship the Lord preceded the proclamation of doom. Also, Revelation 14:8 analogizes the government of the beast to the Neo-Babylonian Empire.

REVELATION 15

Revelation 15 describes seven angels preparing to deliver the seven last plagues that complete God's wrath. The angels of wrath wore shining linen and a gold sash around their chest. Also, all believers slain by the government of the beast went to heaven. They held harps given to them by God and sang a victorious song while proclaiming that all nations will worship the God.

REVELATION 16

Revelation 16 describes the seven angels of wrath pouring out their "bowls" of wrathful plague:

1. The first bowl of wrath gave festering sores to everybody who accepted the mark of the beast. (Revelation 16:2)

2. The second bowl of wrath turned the sea into blood like a dead person. (Revelation 16:3)

3. The third bowl of wrath turned rivers and springs of water into blood. (Revelation 16:4–7)

4. The fourth bowl of wrath made the sun scorch people with fire, but people refused to repent to God who controlled these plagues. (Revelation 16:8–9)

5. The fifth bowl of wrath plunged the throne of the beast and its kingdom into darkness; the people felt agony from all of the plagues and cursed God, but they refused to repent. (Revelation 16:10–11)

6. The sixth bowl of wrath dried up the great Euphrates river; then three impure spirits appeared, one out of the mouth of the dragon, one out of the mouth of the first beast, and one out of the mouth of the second beast also called *the false prophet;* these impure spirits are demons who go out and gather the kings of the entire earth to battle against God in a place called *Armageddon*.[5] (Revelation 16:12–16)

---

5. Armageddon symbolically refers to the region of Megiddo, Israel.

7. The seventh bowl of wrath included the greatest earthquake in the history of humanity; the great city split into three parts while the nations collapsed, and hundred-pound hailstones fell on people. (Revelation 16:17–21)

REVELATION 17

In Revelation 17:1–2, one of the seven angels in charge of wrath says that he will show the author—that is, John the Revelator, the punishment of the great prostitute who sits by many waters. The kings of the earth committed adultery with her while the inhabitants of the earth intoxicated themselves with the wine of her adultery.

In Revelation 17:3–6, the angel spiritually carried John to a wilderness. John saw a woman sitting on a scarlet beast that was covered with blasphemous names and had seven heads and ten horns. The woman wore purple and scarlet clothing, and glittered with gold, precious stones, and pearls. She held a golden cup that was filled with abominations and the filth of her adulteries. She had a mysterious name written on her head: "BABYLON THE GREAT: THE MOTHER OF PROSTITUTES: AND OF THE ABOMINATIONS OF THE EARTH." John saw that the woman was drunk from the blood of God's holy people who bore the testimony of Jesus.

In Revelation 17:6–8, John felt astonished by the sight of the woman, but the angel questioned John's astonishment. The angel also said that he would explain the mystery of the woman and the beast that she rides, which has seven heads and ten horns. The angel said that the beast seen by John previously existed, currently does not exist, and eventually will come up from the Abyss and go to its destruction. The inhabitants of the earth who do not follow Jesus will feel astonished when they see the beast reappear after ceasing to exist.

In Revelation 17:9–11, the angel interprets the following: (1) The seven heads of the beast are the Seven Hills of Rome where the woman sits; (2) the seven heads are also seven kings, five previously existed, one currently exists, and one is yet to come; (3) the beast who previously existed, ceased to exist, and then reappears is an eighth king who belongs to the seven and is going to his destruction.

In Revelation 17:12–14, the angel interprets that the ten horns of the beast are ten kings who do not yet rule a kingdom but for one hour will receive the authority of kingship along with the beast. The ten kings have one purpose and give their power and authority to the beast. They wage war against Christ the Lamb, but the Lamb triumphs over the kings because he is the Lord of lords and King of kings, while all of his chosen and faithful followers are with him.

In Revelation 17:15-18, the angel tells John that the waters seen near the prostitute are the multitudes of people from all nations and languages. The beast and the ten horns hate the prostitute. They ruin her, leave her naked, eat her flesh, and burn her with fire. God determined the hearts of the ten kings to give their royal authority to the beast until God's words are fulfilled. Also, the prostitute is the great city that rules over the kings of the earth.

As discussed earlier, the imagery of the beast represents Rome, a succession of Roman emperors/kings, a final eighth king who comes back to life according the imagery of the Nero redivivus legend, and ten subordinate kings who serve the final king. A murderous prostitute dressed in luxury sits on this beast, while the prostitute is called *Babylon the Great,* which associates the beast with imagery of both Rome and Babylon. The symbolism overlaps because in one context both the beast and the prostitute represent Rome while in another context the beast is distinct from the prostitute. In fact, the beast eventually ruins and burns the prostitute with fire, which might refer to the rumors of Nero causing the Great Fire of Rome.

REVELATION 18

Revelation 18 prophesies judgments from angels and laments from the inhabitants of the nations:

1. An angel with great authority appears and illuminates the earth while his mighty voice begins a proclamation by saying, "Fallen! Fallen is Babylon the Great!" (Revelation 18:1-3)

2. Another voice from heaven called the people of God to come out of Babylon before the final wrath of plagues overtakes it. (Revelation 18:4-8)

3. Inhabitants of the nations lament over the fall of Babylon. (Revelation 18:9-20)

4. A mighty angel proclaims the complete destruction of Babylon. (Revelation 18:21-24)

SELECTIONS FROM REVELATION 19

Revelation 19 describes praise in heaven and the return of the Lord. Multitudes in heaven praise God and pronounce the condemnation of Babylon while proclaiming that the smoke from the burned ruins of Babylon rise for ever and ever. Then, Jesus returns to earth as the "King of kings and Lord of lords" with his heavenly armies. The beast and the kings of the earth with their armies gather to wage war against the Lord. The beast and his false prophet (the second beast) are captured and "thrown alive into the fiery lake of burning sulfur." The kings of the earth and their armies are killed.

This battle between the Lord with his armies and the beast with his armies is the Battle of Armageddon referred to after the sixth bowl of wrath in Revelation 16. Ironically, only one verse—that is, Revelation 20:20, records the capture and punishment of the beast during this infamous battle.

REVELATION 20:1-10

In Revelation 20:1–7, an angel from heaven carries a great chain and the keys to the Abyss while he captures the devil, binds him for 1,000 years, throws him into the Abyss, and locks the Abyss. Then, all believers killed by the beast came back to life and reign with Christ on earth for 1,000 years.

In Revelation 20:8–10, after the 1,000-year reign, the devil ascends from the Abyss to deceive and gather the nations—Gog and Magog—to fight against the Lord. The devil gathers a multitude of people who march across the earth and surround God's people in Jerusalem. But fire comes down from the sky and devours the armies of the devil, and the devil is thrown into the lake of burning sulfur, along with the beast and false prophet. They suffer torment day and night for ever and ever.

The great chain, the Abyss, and everlasting punishment in fire refer to 1 Enoch's imagery of punishment for fallen angels.[6] Also, as mention in chapter 7, "Gog and Magog" refers to the prophecy in Ezekiel 38–39. Moreover, this battle after the 1,000-year reign analogizes the Battle of Armageddon.

The 1,000-year/millennial reign in Revelation 20:1–7 portrays a special resurrection and reign for Christian martyrs killed by the beast.

---

6. See chapter 10 and 1 Enoch 10:11–14 and 54.

The predominant futurist interpretation of this reign is called *premillennialism*, which typically teaches the following:

1. Christ returns and begins the millennial reign.[7]
2. An archangel binds and banishes the devil for the duration of the millennial reign.
3. The millennial reign includes not only resurrected martyrs killed by the beast but all believers who experienced the resurrection and rapture.
4. The millennial reign is literally or rounded to 1,000 years—for example, between 500 and 1,499 years.
5. The millennial reign ends with the reappearance of the devil that precedes the final judgment and the beginning of the new heavens with the new earth.

I propose caution instead of dogmatism when interpreting the apocalyptic picture of the devil's banishment and the reign of Christ with his resurrected martyrs. I also propose that this millennial reign is a minor point instead of a central point in end-time theology. For example, in any case, Christ reigns forever. This paper for the sake of simplification considers two cases: (1) Christ reigns forever during a succession of ages while the future millennial reign is one of those ages; (2) Christ returns and reigns forever in a single everlasting age while there is no future millennial reign. I lean toward the former and see that the 1,000 years is figurative for a long period of time, while nobody could definitively rule out that this long period of time might range from 500 to 1,499 years.

DISCUSSION ON THE BEAST AND CONDITIONAL FUTURISM

This discussion focuses on the nature of the beast and conditional futurism. Any futurist model of the beast's nature could work with conditional futurism, while I also propose that the eighth king is an individual human who portrays the final beast in Revelation 19 during the Battle of Armageddon. This human is the final antichrist and ends up in the fiery lake with the false prophet and the devil.

---

7. Premillennialism means that Christ returns *before* the beginning of the millennium.

Revelation 20:10 pictures the devil, the beast, and the false prophet suffering torment forever in the fiery lake. This portrays a trinity of evil suffering for their evil deeds. This portrait might also suggest that the beast and false prophet are the same nature as the devil. For example, the beast and false prophet might be archdemons who incarnated into archdemon humans—that is, archdemon-human hypostatic unions comparable to the fallen human angelophanies discussed in the chapter 13 section on 1 Peter 3:19–20.[8] However, one big difference between the fallen human angelophanies in 1 Peter and the beast is that the fallen human angelophanies presumably were good when they first turned into humans while the beast would already be an archdemon when he turns into a human.

Other options for the final beast include that he is a mere human possessed by an archdemon, which does not fit the picture of Revelation 20:10. Another option for the beast includes that he is an archdemon masquerading as a human but without a human nature, which does not fit the imagery of the beast arising from the sea in Revelation 13:1–4 while the sea represents humanity. However, sound biblical interpretation may not insist upon dogmatic interpretation of apocalyptic symbolism when no other biblical passages clearly teach a doctrine, so the proposal of the beast as an archdemon human may only be confirmed when the final beast arrives. Incidentally, an incarnation of an archdemon would not require an archdemon father or mother, but God according to his purposes would sovereignly allow the respective archdemon to incarnate in cooperation with an otherwise normal human conception.

The proposal of an archdemon-human antichrist raises the controversy of conditional futurism. For example, according to chapter 1, principles of prophecy found throughout the Old Testament indicate that the final antichrist may read about his doom in Revelation and decide to repent while avoiding that prophetic doom. The antichrist reconciles with Christ and likewise is no longer an antichrist. He decides against leading the opposition to the Lord in the Battle of Armageddon, but becomes a postfiguration of repentant Babylonian king Nebuchadnezzar. This is an option that would fulfill the prophetic purposes of the apoca-

---

8. I introduced this model of the beast/antichrist in "Orthodoxy and Gregory of Nyssa's Universalism," *TheoPerspectives* (blog), October 31, 2007, http://theoperspectives.blogspot.com/2007/10/orthodoxy-and-gregory-of-nyssas.html.

lypse. Moreover, in the case of an archdemon-human antichrist, then an archdemon could repent and reconcile with Christ.

This scenario works fine with Gregory of Nyssa who said:

> The Apostle adds to the number of the "things under the earth," signifying in that passage that when evil shall have been some day annihilated in the long revolutions of the ages, nothing shall be left outside the world of goodness, but that even from those evil spirits confession of Christ's Lordship.[9]

Gregory in *The Great Catechism* also said,

> He [Christ] accomplished all the results before mentioned, freeing both man from evil, and healing even the introducer of evil himself.[10]

In the above quotes, Gregory taught that demons and the devil himself could reconcile with Christ. However, many contemporary churches strongly reject that any demon could convert to Christ under any circumstance.

Augustine in *The City of God* also strongly rejected that the devil or fallen angels of any rank could experience prolonged punishment and then salvation.[11] Augustine said that the church had not tolerated the idea of fallen angels converting back to holy angels, while he implied that the Old and New Testaments rejected the possibility of anything but literal endless punishment for fallen angels. However, Augustine in his letter to Evodius and in all of his other known writings never settled on an interpretation of 1 Peter 3:18–19 teaching about Christ's proclamation to imprisoned spirits, which was imagery of Christ preaching to a class of fallen angels.[12]

Regardless of the controversy, Gregory of Nyssa's view of fallen angels ("evil spirits") was an orthodox option in the ancient church. For example, as mentioned in chapter 13, Emperor Justinian in the AD 553 Fifth Ecumenical Council honored Gregory by calling him a holy father, while Justinian ironically honored Gregory and Augustine side by

---

9. Gregory of Nyssa, "On the Soul and the Resurrection," in *Select Writings*.

10. Gregory of Nyssa, *The Great Catechism*, chapter 26, in *Select Writings*.

11. See Augustine, *The City of God,* Book 21: "Of the Eternal Punishment," chapter 23: "Against Those Who are of Opinion that the Punishment."

12. See chapter 13 and Augustine, *Letters of St. Augustin,* Letter 164.

side as holy fathers.[13] Also, Gregory championed the fourth-century AD Nicene-Constantinople Creed that explicitly taught about Christ returning to judge the living and the dead. This indicates that Gregory's view of demons and the devil possibly reconciling with Christ harmoniously incorporates with the ancient creedal teachings about Christ returning with judgment. Likewise, when Augustine said that the church never tolerated views of fallen angels possibly converting back to holy angels, he neglected to address Gregory's *Great Catechism*. Similarly, my biblical proposal for the possible repentance and salvation of an archdemon-human antichrist fits within the historic boundaries of orthodox Christianity.

Regardless of the correct model of the antichrist, the most practical and urgent point of conditional futurism is that the church needs to pray for the salvation of any possible antichrist. For example, 1 Timothy 2:1–4:

> [1] I urge, then, first of all, that petitions, prayers, intercession and thanksgiving be made for all people— [2] for kings and all those in authority, that we may live peaceful and quiet lives in all godliness and holiness. [3] This is good, and pleases God our Savior, [4] who wants all people to be saved and to come to a knowledge of the truth. (1 Timothy 2:1–4)

First Timothy 2:1–4 urged Christians in the Roman Empire to pray for the emperor and all other Roman authorities, so the church would live in peace and all people including the emperor would enjoy salvation. Ironically, these verses urged Christians to pray for Roman officials including the emperor while Revelation portrayed Roman officials as the enemy of Christ and his church. In fact, the traditional date for the writing of 1 Timothy 2:1–4 was during the reign of Emperor Nero—that is, a model of the final beast, while Christ's primary concern for Nero and all other emperors was their salvation. Likewise, all modern day speculation of who might be an antichrist or the final antichrist requires major prayer for the their salvation. God loves all people and wants all people to enjoy salvation.

---

13. See Percival, *The Seven Ecumenical Councils,* "The Fifth Ecumenical Council."

15

Judgment, the Kings of the Earth, and the Nations in Revelation

THIS FINAL CHAPTER LOOKS at judgment, the kings of the earth, and the nations in Revelation.

JUDGMENT IN REVELATION

Notable judgments in Revelation include the judgment of Babylon,[1] the judgment of the beast and his armies when the Lord returns,[2] judgments during the 1,000-year reign,[3] the judgment of the devil and his armies after the 1,000-year reign,[4] and the judgment of the dead at the great white throne.[5] Also, references to "Hades" indicate that each person faces judgment when they die, while Hades goes into the lake of fire after judgment at the great white throne.[6]

Revelation 14:6–11 evidently conflates the imagery of the fall of Babylon with the return of the Lord and judgment at the great white throne. For example, angels in verses 14:6–8 declare that the hour of judgment has come for Babylon, while verses 14:9–11 pronounce that anybody who worships the beast and accepts his mark will suffer torment day and night from burning sulfur while the smoke of their torment rises forever. This imagery of torment day and night in burning sulfur is then mentioned in the following: (1) verse 19:20 when the beast

---

1. Revelation 14:6—19:3.
2. Revelation 19:11–21.
3. Revelation 20:4.
4. Revelation 20:7–10.
5. Revelation 20:11–15.
6. Revelation 1:18 and 20:13–14.

and false prophet are thrown into the fiery lake of burning sulfur after the return of the Lord, (2) verse 20:10 when the devil joins the beast and false prophet in the lake of burning sulfur where they suffer torment day and night forever, and (3) verses 20:14–15 when all of the unsaved are thrown into the lake of fire after the white throne judgment. Likewise, the imagery of the lake of fire with burning sulfur focuses more on theme instead of chronology, while verse 19:20 pictures final judgment for the beast and false prophet, verse 20:10 pictures final judgment for the devil, and verses 20:14–15 pictures final judgment for all unsaved humans in Hades.

The Lord's return with the beast confined to the lake of fire corresponds to the events in 2 Thessalonians 2, which says that the Lord will return and destroy the man of lawlessness. Also, Revelation 20:4 says that believers killed by the beast resurrect after the Lord's return and reign with the Lord for 1,000 years. This resurrection corresponds to the resurrection in 1 Thessalonians 4:13–18, which says all dead believers will resurrect when the Lord returns. Likewise, the resurrection in Revelation 20:4 may symbolically refer to the resurrection of all dead believers while making special honor to the martyrs. Additionally, verse 20:4 refers to thrones of judgment, which might involve the judgment of believers described in 1 Corinthians 3:10–15.[7]

THE KINGS IN REVELATION

Revelation presents a complex view of the kings of the earth/world; in summary:

1. Jesus Christ rules the kings of the earth, and freed all believers from theirs sins by his shed blood. (Revelation 1:5).

2. The kings of the earth hide in caves to dodge the wrath of God. (Revelation 6:15)

3. An angel told the author John the Revelator, "You must prophesy again about many peoples, nations, languages and kings." (Revelation 10:11)

---

7. See chapter 12 for discussion of 2 Thessalonians 2, 1 Thessalonians 4:13–18, and 1 Corinthians 3:10–15.

4. Believers killed by the beast hold harps given to them by God and proclaim that all nations will worship before the Lord. (Revelation 15:2–4)

5. The kings of the whole world gather at Armageddon to battle against God. (Revelation 16:12–16)

6. The kings of the earth participate in the evil ways of the great prostitute—that is, Babylon. (Revelation 17:2)

7. The ten horns of the beast represent ten kings who for one hour rule with authority along with the beast. (Revelation 17:12)

8. The great prostitute represents Babylon that rules over the kings of the earth. (Revelation 17:18)

9. Angels pronounce the fall and smoldering of Babylon while the kings of the earth cry. (Revelation 18:9)

10. An angel standing in the sun shouted to the birds in the air for them to gather together and "eat the dead bodies of kings, generals, and other mighty people." (Revelation 19:17–18)

11. The beast and the kings of the earth with their armies gather to battle against the returning Lord. (Revelation 19:19)

12. The Lord returns with his army; the beast and false prophet are captured and thrown into the fiery lake of burning sulfur; a sword kills the rest, which are the kings and their armies; birds gorge on the dead bodies. (Revelation 19:20–21)

13. The dead face the judgment of God at the great white throne; all people not found in the book of life are thrown into the lake of fire that burns with sulfur. (Revelation 20:11–15)

14. The nations walk by the light of the city of New Jerusalem; the kings of the world bring their glory into the city; the city gates never shut; nothing impure enters the city gates, but only people found written in the book of life enter the city. (Revelation 21:24–27)

Complexity of the kings in Revelation includes that Revelation 1:5 says that Christ rules the kings of the earth while verse 17:8 says that the prostitute rules the kings of the earth. This paradox indicates Christ's ultimate sovereignty over evil entities such as the prostitute and the kings under her rule.

Another paradox of the kings in Revelation involves their transition from enemies of Christ to inhabiting heaven. After the declaration of Christ's rulership in Revelation 1:5, then every mention of "kings" through Revelation 20 is negative; for example, the kings fearfully hide in caves; they gather for the Battle of Armageddon; they commit evil with the prostitute; they rule with the beast; they cry at the smoldering of the prostitute; they die during the Lord's return and the Battle of Armageddon; all not found in the book of life are thrown into the lake of fire. In the midst of all these evil accounts, verses 15:2–4 proclaim that all nations will worship the Lord, which evidently includes that the kings of the nations will worship the Lord. But nonetheless, all the action of the kings in Revelation 6–20 is evil and ends with their slaughter at Armageddon. Then, the kings next appear in verse 21:24 when the kings bring their glory into the New Jerusalem, which is imagery of heaven.

This paradoxical juxtaposition of "the kings" rebelling and then dying at Armageddon versus "the kings" entering heaven suggests that at least some of the kings opposing the Lord to their death would eventually enter heaven.[8] For example, the most natural interpretation of verse 21:24 is that these kings in heaven include at least some of the kings in Revelation 16–20, who plotted Armageddon and died during the Lord's return. In fact, only a strained interpretation of Revelation would conclude that none of the kings in verse 21:24 were among the kings in Revelation 16–20.

The apocalyptic picture of kings dying at Armageddon and entering heaven indicates the possibility of postmortem conversions. The gates of heaven never shut while only the pure enter those gates. Also, as documented in chapter 13, belief in postmortem conversions during the descent of Christ into hell and afterwards was a popular doctrine and accepted as orthodox in the ancient church. Moreover, this indicates that Peter and John the Revelator taught about postmortem conversions.

Conditional futurism does not require this interpretation of the kings in heaven. But given this interpretation, Revelation 22:14–15 teaches about the conditions for the salvation of the kings during life or death:

---

8. I proposed this interpretation of Revelation's "kings" in "The Kings of the Earth in Heaven," *TheoPerspectives* (blog), February 3, 2010, http://theoperspectives.blogspot.com/2010/02/kings-earth-heaven.html.

> ¹⁴ Blessed are those who wash their robes, that they may have the right to the tree of life and may go through the gates into the city. ¹⁵ Outside are the dogs, those who practice magic arts, the sexually immoral, the murderers, the idolaters and everyone who loves and practices falsehood. (Revelation 22:14–15)

These verses teach that only those who meet the condition of washing their robes may enter through the gates of heaven, while "wash their robes" symbolically refers to accepting divine cleansing from sin. Also, Revelation 1:5 teaches that believers are forgiven of their sins by the shed blood of Jesus, which reveals the agency of how the inhabitants of heaven meet the condition of cleansing from sin. Moreover, the phrase *wash their robes* suggests that the believers actively cooperate with their salvation.

OBJECTIONS TO POSTMORTEM CONVERSIONS

This section discusses objections to belief in postmortem conversions in general, while the previous section indicated that Peter and John the Revelator taught about postmortem conversions. For example, Augustine in *City of God,* Book 21, presented the most prominent and influential objections to the belief of postmortem conversions in ancient history;[9] the following selection objects to the worst teaching associated with Origen:

> I must now, I see, enter the lists of amicable controversy with those tender-hearted Christians who decline to believe that any, or that all of those whom the infallibly just Judge may pronounce worthy of the punishment of hell, shall suffer eternally, and who suppose that they shall be delivered after a fixed term of punishment, longer or shorter according to the amount of each man's sin. In respect of this matter, Origen was even more indulgent; for he believed that even the devil himself and his angels, after suffering those more severe and prolonged pains which their sins deserved, should be delivered from their torments, and associated with the holy angels. But the Church, not without reason, condemned him for this and other errors, especially for his theory of the ceaseless alternation of happiness and misery, and the interminable transitions from the one state to the other at fixed periods of ages; for in this theory he lost even the credit

---

9. Chapter 13 briefly mentioned some of these objections in the discussion of postmortem conversions during the descent of Christ.

of being merciful, by allotting to the saints real miseries for the expiation of their sins, and false happiness, which brought them no true and secure joy, that is, no fearless assurance of eternal blessedness.[10]

Augustine in the above quote acknowledged that many of his fellow Christians believed that all or some people in hell endure temporary punishments while eventually enjoying salvation. As previously mentioned, he referred to various beliefs of temporary punishments in hell as an "amicable controversy" within the orthodox church. However, Augustine said that the church condemned Origen and his followers for teaching that the devil and his angels would eventually enjoy salvation while the worst heresy associated with Origenism was the teaching that saints would forever alternate between periods of misery and happiness. This worst heresy implied that saints would forever suffer periods of misery with no assurance of everlasting joy, while misery without God's mercy resulted in the forgiveness of sins. I agree with Augustine that belief in temporary punishments in hell was a friendly controversy in the church and belief in an endless series of periodic misery that pays for sins is a terrible doctrine. However, no historical record indicates that the ancient church ever condemned Gregory of Nyssa for teaching about the salvation of the devil in his *Great Catechism*,[11] so Origenist versions of the devil's eventual salvation were condemned but not Gregory's teaching. Likewise, Augustine apparently misinterpreted church history in regards to the possibility of the devil's salvation. Also, Augustine refuted *all* versions of postmortem conversions but condemned only *some* of the versions.

Augustine in *City of God*, Book 21, also distinguished between some departed believers who needed temporary purging versus departed unbelievers facing inescapable everlasting hell.[12] The teaching of some departed believers needing temporary purging eventually developed into the medieval Roman Catholic doctrine of purgatory. Ironically, numerous people in personal communication suggested to me that the ancient church teaching of temporary punishments in hell was the doctrine of

---

10. Augustine, *The City of God,* Book 21: "Of the Eternal Punishment," chapter 17: "Of Those Who Fancy that No Men."

11. Gregory of Nyssa, *The Great Catechism,* chapter 26, in *Select Writings*.

12. Augustine, *The City of God,* Book 21: "Of the Eternal Punishment," chapter 26: "What It is to Have Christ."

purgatory, but church history indicates that the doctrine of purgatory developed after the doctrine of temporary punishments in hell while Augustine made a clear distinction between the two doctrines.

Augustine in *City of God,* Book 21, additionally objected to the possibility of God saving all or some people in hell (postmortem conversions) because such a possibility would weaken the church's faith in the everlasting punishment of the devil and his fallen angels.[13] I find trouble with Augustine's logic in this, while I am unsure of the context. Perhaps he misunderstood Origenism and supposed that it taught about evil angels eventually causing havoc in heaven. But Origen taught that the entity named the devil, symbolically represented as death, would inhabit heaven only after the destruction of the devil's evil nature.[14] Another possible respective logic of Augustine is that he despised the possibility of the devil and other evil angels eventually repenting and rediscovering the favor of God, which I hope was not Augustine's Christian motivation. Or perhaps Augustine and the church condemned Origenist teaching that said the devil would forever alternate between good periods and evil periods, which was a terrible teaching.

Augustine in *City of God,* Book 21, moreover looked at the comparison of "eternal punishment" and "eternal life" in Matthew 25:41–46. He argued that the eternal punishment and the eternal life are correlative. Likewise, he insisted that the duration of eternal punishment must equal the duration of eternal life; they both could be long periods of time with an end or endless, but one cannot be a long period with an end while the other is endless.[15]

I agree that the imagery for the duration of "eternal punishment" appears equivalent to the imagery for the duration of "eternal life."[16] However, the context of the two drastically differs. For example, all rewards of eternal punishment are deserved while eternal life is undeserved favor. Also, God desires to save all people while leaving none in hell. Additionally, God's primary purpose for punishment is not endless punishment but loving correction. Besides, the parabolic form of Matthew 25:31–46 suggests a symbolic interpretation while Peter and

13. See Augustine, *The City of God,* Book 21: "Of the Eternal Punishment," chapter 23: "Against Those Who are of Opinion that the Punishment."

14. Origen, *De Principiis,* Book 3, chapter 6:5.

15. See Augustine, *The City of God,* Book 21, chapter 23.

16. See chapter 11.

John the Revelator taught about postmortem conversions. Likewise, the context challenges a rigid correlation for the duration of eternal punishment and eternal life.

As mentioned in chapter 13, another famous ancient objection to postmortem conversions occurred during the AD 553 Fifth Ecumenical Council. Emperor Justinian ironically honored Gregory of Nyssa and Augustine as revered church fathers while condemning Origen.

Recent controversies about faith in the possibility of postmortem conversions involve Carlton Pearson and Rob Bell. For example, Pearson in 2008 wrote *The Gospel of Inclusion* and Bell in 2011 wrote *Love Wins*.

The Joint College of African-American Pentecostal Bishops Congress in 2004 denounced Carlton as a heretic.[17] Pearson went from traditional Pentecostalism to inclusivist universalism. He teaches that Christ died for everybody, so everybody is *automatically* saved while faith in Christ is *optional* for salvation. This gospel of inclusion teaches a radical view of universalism that is incompatible with conditional futurism, which insists upon the condition of faith in Christ for salvation.

Rob Bell is a megachurch pastor and author who recently stirred controversy with his 2011 book *Love Wins: A Book About Heaven, Hell, and the Fate of Every Person Who Ever Lived*. Bell sticks with the biblical tradition that faith in Christ is required for salvation while Bell suggests the possibility of this salvation for the damned in hell, which as previously indicated is doctrine that is compatible with orthodox Christianity including the Nicene-Constantinople Creed. However, fierce opponents of Bell such as Albert Mohler misrepresent Bell and church history while saying that Bell promotes "the denial of hell."[18] Regardless of the misrepresentation, Bell's view of heaven and hell is compatible with the Bible and conditional futurism.

I face other objections to postmortem conversions in personal communication. Some say that hearers of the gospel might avoid repenting if they believe in a temporary hell. Others imply that commitment to the great commission of evangelizing the world is meaningless if the offer of salvation extends to the damned in hell.

A doctrine of no postmortem punishments would plausibly encourage many people to avoid repentance and following Christ. But conditional futurism clearly teaches that postmortem punishments are

---

17. Gaines, "Black Pentecostal Group Denounces Carlton Pearson as a Heretic."
18. Mohler, "Why so Serious."

proportional to the level of sin according to Christ's teachings about judgment in the Gospels. Divine punishment for knowledgeable and willful disobedience is harsh, regardless that the punishment might end. Also, all must cleanse themselves from sin through Christ to enter heaven, in this life or the afterlife.

Concerning the evangelization of the world, I feel astonished that some lovers of Christ suggest that they would disobey Christ and let the world go to hell if Christ would attempt to reach the supposedly billions of lost souls in hell. Christ taught us to pray for the Father's kingdom to come on earth as it is in heaven. Lovers of Christ should never consider disobeying him by neglecting to work toward the establishment of God's kingdom on earth because of his everlasting love and desire for everybody's salvation. If some believers make decisions based not on direction from God but in response to the Western Christian interpretation of inescapable hell, then such decisions needs reconsideration while the church remains committed to obeying God and evangelizing the world until every soul is saved.

I also face controversy because of biblical belief in the possibility of postmortem conversions. I needed to resign my ministry credentials from a Pentecostal denomination before I could freely teach my recently modified end-time theology. This continues to limit the number of local charismatic and Pentecostal churches that would allow me in their membership and leadership. However, my urgent pastoral and philosophical concern is that I can no longer suggest that there is no possible hope for loved ones who departed without Christ. This includes my rejection that there is no possible hope for billions of people who already died lost and suffer literal endless torment. Such hopelessness conflicts with the overall message of the Bible, while the Bible never teaches such hopelessness.

CONDITIONAL FUTURISM AND THE NATIONS IN REVELATION

Revelation uses the word *nations* seventeen times:

1. Victorious Christians acquire divine authority to rule the nations. (Revelation 2:26 and 12:5)

2. John the Revelator must prophesy to the nations. (Revelation 10:11)

3. The wrath of God comes against angry nations. (Revelation 11:18)
4. Babylon made the nations drunk from maddening wine. (Revelation 14:8 and 18:3)
5. The saints killed by the beast hold harps and declare that the Lord God is the just King of the nations. (Revelation 15:4)
6. The saints killed by the beast prophesy that all nations will come and worship before the Lord. (Revelation 15:5)
7. The seventh/final bowl of wrath causes the nations to collapse. (Revelation 16:19)
8. The prostitute sits near waters that represent the nations. (Revelation 17:15)
9. The prostitute led the nations astray. (Revelation 18:23)
10. Christ returns and strikes down the nations. (Revelation 19:15)
11. An angel binds the devil and banishes him into the Abyss for 1,000 years so he can no longer deceive the nations. (Revelation 20:3)
12. The devil reappears from the Abyss to again deceive the nations; he gathers the nations to attack God's people, but fire devours the attacking nations. (Revelation 20:8–9)
13. The nations walk by the light of the New Jerusalem and bring their glory and honor into it. (Revelation 21:24–26)
14. The leaves from the tree of life bring healing to the nations. (Revelation 22:2)

The references to the nations in Revelation greatly vary. On one hand, the nations are enemies to God and suffer collapse. On the other hand, the nations come to God and worship him. The progression of the references indicates that the nations convert from disobeying God to glorifying God, which is consistent with the prophecy in Isaiah and Psalms.[19] For example, Richard Bauckham concludes that the conversion of the nations is central to the prophecy in Revelation.[20]

Conditional futurism teaches that God purposes to convert the nations. And the Lord's return could follow various scenarios that range from the rise of a world-dominating antichrist to a worldwide golden

---

19. See chapters 4 and 5.
20. See Bauckham, *Climax of Prophecy*, 238.

age of Christianity. In the case of an unrepentant world-dominating antichrist, the church could look better than common scenarios predicted by pretribulationism.[21] Also, regardless of the decisions of the final antichrist, the last generation of the church may minister to the nations with extraordinary power. For example, the two witnesses in Revelation 11 represent the power of the end-time church. This goes along with Christ in John 14:12 teaching that his followers would replicate his works and even do greater works than Christ did during his earthly ministry.

In conclusion, God commands his children and church to hope for the best in every circumstance while God works all things for the good of those who love him.[22] Likewise, the divine purpose of end-time prophecies encourages hope for all believers in all circumstances.

---

21. See Ladd, *The Blessed Hope*.
22. See Romans 8:18–32.

Bibliography

Alfeyev, Hilarion. "Christ the Conqueror of Hell: The Descent of Christ into Hades in Eastern and Western Theological Traditions." Lecture delivered at St Mary's Cathedral, Minneapolis, Minnesota on November 5, 2002. http://orthodoxeurope.org/page/11/1/5.aspx.

The Apocrypha. http://www.sacred-texts.com/bib/apo/index.htm.

Aquinas, Thomas. *Summa Theologica.* Translated by the Fathers of the English Dominican Province. http://www.ccel.org/ccel/aquinas/summa.i.html.

Augustine. *The City of God.* Translated by Marcus Dods. *A Select Library of the Nicene and Post-Nicene Fathers of the Christian Church: Volume II: St. Augustin's: City of God and Christian Doctrine,* edited by Philip Schaff. http://www.ccel.org/ccel/schaff/npnf102.iv.html.

Augustine. *Letters of St. Augustin.* Translated by J. G. Cunningham. *A Select Library of the Nicene and Post-Nicene Fathers of the Christian Church: Volume I: The Confessions and Letters of St. Augustin, with a Sketch of His Life and Work,* edited by Philip Schaff. http://www.ccel.org/ccel/schaff/npnf101.vii.html.

The Babylonian Talmud. Translated by Michael L. Rodkinson. http://www.sacred-texts.com/jud/talmud.htm.

Balthasar, Hans Urs Von. *Mysterium Paschale: The Mystery of Easter.* Translated by Aidan Nichols. San Francisco: Ignatius Press, 1990.

Bauckham, Richard. *Climax of Prophecy: Studies on the Book of Revelation.* London: T&T Clark, 2000.

Bauckham, Richard, and Trevor A. Hart. *Hope against Hope: Christian Eschatology at the Turn of the Millennium.* Grand Rapids, Michigan: Eerdmans, 1999.

Bell, Rob. *Love Wins: A Book About Heaven, Hell, and the Fate of Every Person Who Ever Lived.* New York: HarperOne, 2011.

Blowers, Paul M. "Apokatastasis." In *The New Westminster Dictionary of Church History, Volume One: The Early, Medieval, and Reformation Eras,* edited by Robert Benedetto, 36–37. Louisville, Kentucky: Westminster John Knox Press, 2008.

Bullinger, E. W. *Number in Scripture: Its Supernatural Design and Spiritual Significance,* 4th edition. London: Eyre & Spottiswoode, 1921. http://www.scribd.com/doc/47333280/Number-in-Scripture-It-s-Supernatural-Design-and-Spiritual-Significance-E-W-Bullinger-1921.

Clement of Alexandria. *The Stromata, or Miscellanies.* Translated by Wilson. In *Ante-Nicene Fathers: Translations of the Writings of the Fathers down to AD 325: Volume II: Fathers of the Second Century: Hermas, Tatian, Athenagoras, Theophilus, and Clement of Alexandria (Entire),* edited by Alexander Roberts, James Donaldson, and A. Cleveland Coxe. http://www.ccel.org/ccel/schaff/anf02.vi.iv.html.

Bibliography

Dickens, Charles. *A Christmas Carol.* http://www.literature.org/authors/dickens-charles/christmas-carol.

Ericson, Norman R. "Spirits in Prison." In *Baker's Evangelical Dictionary of Biblical Theology,* edited by Walter A. Elwell, 745–746. Grand Rapids, Michigan: Baker Book House, 1995.

Gaines, Adrienne S. "Black Pentecostal Group Denounces Carlton Pearson as a Heretic," *Charisma,* June 30, 2004. http://www.charismamag.com/index.php/component/content/article/268-people-and-events/9245-black-pentecostal-group-denounces-carlton-pearson-as-a-heretic.

Gregory of Nyssa. "On the Three-day Period of the Resurrection of Our Lord Jesus Christ." Translated by S. G. Hall. In *Easter Sermons of Gregory of Nyssa,* edited by Andreas Spira and Christoph Klock, 31–50. Cambridge, Massachusetts: Philadelphia Patristic Foundation, 1981.

Gregory of Nyssa. *Select Writings and Letters of Gregory, Bishop of Nyssa.* Translated by William Moore and Henry Austin Wilson. In *A Select Library of the Nicene and Post-Nicene Fathers of the Christian Church: Second Series: Volume V: Gregory of Nyssa: Dogmatic Treatises, Etc.,* edited by Philip Schaff and Henry Wace. http://www.ccel.org/ccel/schaff/npnf205.iii.html.

Hodge, Charles. *Systematic Theology: Volume II.* Grand Rapids, Michigan: Eerdmans, 1940. http://www.ccel.org/ccel/hodge/theology2.html.

Irenaeus. *Against Heresies.* Translated by Roberts and Rambaut. In *Ante-Nicene Fathers: Translations of the Writings of the Fathers down to AD 325: Volume I: The Apostolic Fathers, Justin Martyr, Irenaeus,* edited by Alexander Roberts, James Donaldson, and A. Cleveland Coxe. http://www.ccel.org/ccel/schaff/anf01.ix.html.

Josephus, Flavius. *The Wars of the Jews.* Translated by William Whiston. http://www.sacred-texts.com/jud/josephus/index.htm#woj.

Kearley, F. Furman. "The Conditional Nature of Prophecy: A Vital Exegetical and Hermeneutical Principle." Last modified January 28, 2004. Apologetics Press. http://www.apologeticspress.org/rr/reprints/Conditional-Nature-of-Prophecy.pdf.

Ladd, George Eldon. *The Blessed Hope: A Biblical Study of the Second Advent and the Rapture.* Grand Rapids, Michigan: Eardmans, 1990.

Ladd, George Eldon. *The Presence of the Future: The Eschatology of Biblical Realism.* Grand Rapids, Michigan: Eardmans, 1996.

LaSor, William Sanford, et al. *Old Testament Survey: The Message, Form, and Background of the Old Testament,* 2nd edition. Grand Rapids: Eerdmans, 1996.

Mohler, R. Albert. "Why so Serious? Taking the Gospel Seriously Demands Taking Hell Seriously." *Southern Seminary Magazine* 79, Summer (2011): 26–30. http://www.sbts.edu/resources/files/2011/06/ssm_summer-2011_web.pdf.

Moltmann, Jurgen. "Descent into Hell." Translated by M. Douglas Meeks. *The Duke Divinity School Review* 33 (1968): 115–119.

Myers, Steven Lee. "Babylon Ruins Reopen in Iraq, to Controversy," *New York Times,* May 3, 2009. http://www.nytimes.com/2009/05/03/world/middleeast/03babylon.html.

Nickelsburg, George W. E., and James C. VanderKam, translator. *1 Enoch: A New Translation.* Minneapolis: Fortress Press, 2004. http://www.scribd.com/doc/42050904/Enoch-A-New-Translation-NickelsBurg-and-Vanderkam.

Origen. *De Principiis.* Translated by Frederick Crombie. In *Ante-Nicene Fathers: Translations of the Writings of the Fathers down to AD 325: Volume IV: Fathers of the*

Third Century: Tertullian, Part Fourth; Minucius Felix; Commodian; Origen, Parts First and Second, edited by A. Cleveland Coxe. http://www.ccel.org/ccel/schaff/anf04.vi.v.i.html.

Pearson, Carlton. *The Gospel of Inclusion: Reaching Beyond Religious Fundamentalism to the True Love of God and Self.* New York: Atria Books, 2008.

Percival, Henry R., compiler. *The Seven Ecumenical Councils of the Undivided Church.* http://www.ccel.org/ccel/schaff/npnf214.toc.html.

Ramm, Bernard. *Protestant Biblical Interpretation: A Textbook of Hermeneutics,* 3rd edition. Grand Rapids, Michigan: Baker Book House, 1970.

Talbott, Thomas. "A Pauline Interpretation of Divine Judgment." In *Universal Salvation?: The Contemporary Debate,* edited by Robin Parry and Christopher Partridge. Grand Rapids, Michigan: Eerdmans, 2004.

Walvoord, John F. *The Rapture Question,* Revised edition. Grand Rapids: Zondervan, 1979.

Subject Index

abomination, 75–81, 106–108, 112, 145, 149

angel, 8, 13, 35, 51, 56–57, 68–69, 71, 75, 79–82, 85–87, 92–93, 95, 103, 106–107, 112–115, 118, 120,125–127, 132, 135–140, 142, 144–158, 160–162, 165

angelophany, 13, 137–140, 153

antichrist, 5, 35, 52, 65, 67, 82, 129–130, 132, 141–142, 144, 152–155, 165–166

antichrists, 101, 132, 141, 144

Antiochus IV Epiphanes, 69, 73–74, 76–77, 80–82, 108, 129, 145

apocalypse, 1–3, 5, 8, 13, 55–58, 61, 65–67, 69, 72, 77, 80–82, 86, 136, 138–139, 143–145, 152–153, 159

apocatastasis, 134–136

archangel. *See* angel

archdemon. *See* demon.

Augustine, 134–137, 154–155, 160–163

Babylon, 2, 7, 14, 17, 21, 23, 28, 33–52, 55, 58, 61–77, 80, 88–89, 144, 147–151, 153, 156–158, 165

beast, 1, 6, 52, 64–70, 140, 143–59, 165

covenant, 5, 13–18, 21–23, 29, 32, 46–47, 75, 78, 80, 110, 119

Descent of Christ into Hell, 133–136, 159–160

demon, 91–93, 102–103, 121, 138, 140, 145, 148, 153–155

devil, 11–12, 35, 40, 51–52, 56–57, 85, 93, 114–115, 128–129, 142, 145, 151–157, 160–162, 165

eighth king, 5–6, 52, 70, 143–155

fallen angel, 86–87, 136–138, 140, 146, 151, 154–155, 162

Fifth Ecumenical Council, 135, 154–155, 163

Fourth Ecumenical Council, 139

Gog, 48–54, 151

Gregory of Nyssa, 134–137, 153–155, 161, 163

Hades, 92, 95–96, 133, 156–157

Harrowing of Hell. *See* Descent of Christ into Hell.

hell, 7, 40–41, 93, 102–103, 109–111, 115–116, 133–136, 159–164

hypostatic union, 139, 153

Jerusalem, 7, 19, 21, 26, 29–31, 37–39, 42–46, 52, 55–60, 65, 67, 71, 73–77, 80, 93–94, 98–102, 104–105, 107–108, 110–111, 116–118, 145, 151, 158–159, 165

kingdom of God, 5, 7, 65, 69–70, 82–86, 92–94, 96–97, 100–101, 103, 109–110, 117–118, 124, 140

kingdom of heaven. *See* kingdom of God.

kings of the earth, 6, 21–22, 24–27, 34, 39, 44, 51, 99, 101, 105, 143, 148–151, 155–159

kings of the whole world. *See* kings of the earth.

kings over nations. *See* kings of the earth.

man of lawlessness, 5, 128–129, 144, 157

Nephilim, 13, 136–139

Mount of Olives, 59–60, 98–102, 104–108, 111–115

nations, 4, 16, 20, 23–27, 29–30, 33–34, 37, 39, 43–47, 49–52, 59, 68, 78, 99, 101, 103, 105, 107, 111–114, 120, 145–151, 156–166

Nebuchadnezzar, vi, 2–3, 8, 17, 21, 30, 43–46, 48, 55, 62–67, 75, 144, 153
Neo-Babylonian Empire. *See* Babylon.
Nero, 144, 147, 150, 155
Olivet. *See* Mount of Olives.
Onias III, 73–74, 76-77, 82
Roman Empire. *See* Rome.
Rome, 6–7, 36, 65, 69–70, 77, 83, 100–102, 107, 123, 136, 143–145, 149–50, 155
Satan. *See* devil.
spirits, 34, 132–140, 148, 154

Author Index

Alfeyev, Hilarion, 133, 136
Aquinas, Thomas, 133
Augustine, 134–137, 154–155, 160–163
Balthasar, Hans Urs Von, 136
Bauckham, Richard, 144, 165
Bell, Rob, 163
Blowers, Paul M., 134
Bullinger, E. W., 76, 143
Clement of Alexandria, 133
Dickens, Charles, vi
Ericson, Norman R., 138
Gaines, Adrienne S., 163
Gregory of Nyssa, 134–136, 154–155, 161, 163
Hart, Trevor A., 144
Hodge, Charles, 136
Irenaeus, 133, 135, 137
Josephus, Flavius, 77, 102
Kearley, F. Furman, 1
Ladd, George Eldon, 5, 130, 166
LaSor, William Sanford, 11, 61
Mohler, R. Albert, 163
Moltmann, Jurgen, 136
Myers, Steven Lee, 34
Nickelsburg, George W., 86–87
Origen, 133–136, 160–163
Pearson, Carlton, 163
Percival, Henry R., 135, 139, 155
Ramm, Bernard, 6
Talbott, Thomas, 127
VanderKam, James C., 86–87
Walvoord, John F., 130

Ancient Document Index

OLD TESTAMENT/ HEBREW BIBLE

Genesis

Reference	Page
	5
2:4—3:24	10–11
2:9	10
2:17	10
3:14–15	12
3:14	12
3:15	12
3:19	12
6—9	12–13
6	140
6:1–8	136–138
6:1–4	13, 138–140
6:2	137
6:3	137
6:4	137
6:5–8	137
10:2	48
12	13–4, 16
12:1–3	13–14, 25
12:4–7	14
15	14–6, 25
15:1–6	15
15:7–8	15
15:9–11	15
15:12–16	15
15:17–18	15
17	15–16
17:5	14
18—19	13
18:1—19:25	138
18:16–19:29	28, 92
25:19–34	16
27:1–40	16
29:32—35:18	16
32:22–32	16

Exodus

Reference	Page
	17
13:21—40:38	31
29:38–39	73

Leviticus

Reference	Page
	17
11:4–8	73
16	57
16:2	31

Numbers

Reference	Page
	17
1:1–16	16
9:15—16:42	31
13:31–33	139
25:12–13	17

Deuteronomy

Reference	Page
	17
18:15–19	120

1 Samuel

Reference	Page
8:1—16:13	18
16:1–13	32
16:14—31:13	18

2 Samuel

1:1—5:10	19
7:1–17	19
7:8–16	19
7:12–16	20
11:1—24:25	20

1 Kings

1:1–2:12	20
11:1–13	20
11:9–43	20
11:43—22:53	21
12:1–24	20
12:25—22:53	21

2 Kings

1:1—17:23	21
1:1—25:7	21
17	42
22:1—25:21	43

1 Chronicles

	20

2 Chronicles

	20
9:31—36:21	21
36:15–19	30
36:22–23	37, 75

Ezra

	56
1—6	55
1:1—6:18	30
1:1–4	37, 75
6:1–12	76
6	46
6:14	55
7:11–26	76

Nehemiah

	56
2:1–9	76

Job

38:6–7	35

Psalms

	165
2	24–25
2:1–2	25
2:1–3	24
2:7–8	25
22:27–29	25–26
22:28	26
74:14	147
86:9	26
89	21–24
89:1–4	21
89:5–18, 21	23–24
89:19–37	22–23
89:19–29	23
89:27	23–24
89:30–33	23–24
89:34–37	23
89:38–52	23
89:38–45	24
89:38	24
89:51	24
94:4	84
102:15–16	26
110	26–27, 50
110:1	27, 98
110:1–2	26–27
110:5–6	27

Isaiah

	28, 40, 43, 47, 50, 67, 131, 165
1	28–29
1:7–8	28

Ancient Document Index

Isaiah - continued

1:10	28
1:11–20	28
1:18	28
1:19	28
1:20	28
1:21–29	29
1:31	29, 40
2	37, 39
2:1–5	29–30
2:2	29
2:3	30
2:4	30
4:2–6	30–31, 36–37, 38
9:6–7	30–32
10:5–19	36
11	32
11:1–5	32
11:1	32
11:6–9	32
13:1—14:27	33–35
13—23	33
13:19–20	33
14:3–23	34
14:9–11	34
14:11	40
14:12–15	34–35
14:24–27	36
19	35–37, 39
19:1–17	35
19:18–25	35
19:22–25	35–36
19:22	36
19:23–25	36
23:13	33
27:1	147
30:31	36
31:8–9	36
40:1–5	37, 39
40:1–2	37
40:3–5	37
45:22–25	38
45:22–24	130–131
45:22	38
45:23–24	38
45:23	40
45:24	40
45:25	38
46—47	39
52:13—53:12	30
60:1–3	39
65	39–40
65:1–16	39
65:17–25	39
66:22–24	40, 50
66:22	50
66:24	115

Jeremiah

	67, 74
7	43
18:1–10	2–4, 47
18:7–10	3–4
18:7–8	vi
25	75
25:1–14	45
27	43
27:1–11	4, 44
27:12–15	45
29—33	44
29:4–7	45
30:3	46
31:31–34	46–47
31:32–34	47
31:32	47
31:33	47
31:34	47
46—51	44, 47
46:14	47

Ezekiel

	48
3:18	53
18:21–23	53
33:13–16	2–4
33:14–16	54

33:14–15	vi
38—39	48–54
38:1–6	49
38:7–16	49–50
38:17–23	49
38:19–22	51
39:1–6	49
39:7–8	49
39:9–10	49–50
39:11–20	50
39:17–18	51
39:21–24	50
39:25–29	50

Daniel

	8, 59, 61, 130, 145
1	62
2	61–65, 82
2:1–6	62
2:7–9	62
2:10–13	62
2:14–16	62
2:17–23	63
2:24	63
2:25	63
2:26–47	63–64
2:48–49	64
4	1, 3, 8, 61, 66–67
4:1–18	66
4:9–13	66
4:14-17	66–67
4:18	67
4:19–33	66
4:19–27	2, 66
4:19	67
4:20–27	67
4:27	vi, 3
4:28–37	67
4:34–37	66
7—12	61–82
7	61, 68–69, 82, 147
7:1	61, 68
7:2–7	68
7:8	68
7:9–10	68, 70
7:11	68
7:12	68
7:13–14	68, 70, 85
7:14	70
7:15–18	68
7:19–22	69
7:22	70
7:23–25	69
7:26–27	69
7:27	70
7:28	69
8—12	69
8—9	77, 80
8	70–74, 76, 80
8:1–4	70
8:5–8	70
8:9–12	71
8:13–14	71
8:13	76, 129
8:14	73
8:15–16	71
8:17	71
8:18	71
8:19–26	71–72
8:27	72
9—12	74
9	74–77
9:1–19	74
9:20–27	74–75
9:24	76
9:25	76
9:27	76
10—12	77
10:3—11:1	77, 79
10:40–43	80
11:2–35	80
11:2–4	78
11:5–20	78, 80
11:21–35	78, 80
11:31	76
11:35–45	78
11:36–45	80–81

Daniel - continued

11:36–37	129
11:37	80
12:1–13	78–79
12:1–4	81
12:1	81, 108
12:2–3	85
12:2	85
12:5–13	81
12:7	81
12:11–12	81
12:11	76, 81
12:12	81
12:13	82

Jonah

	4

Zechariah

1:1	55
1:7—6:8	55, 58
1:12–17	46
3	55–56, 58–59
3:1–10	56
4	55, 57, 59
6	58
6:9–15	55, 58–59
6:12–13	58
6:14	58
9—14	55
12—14	55–59
12:1–9	59
12:10–14	59
13	59
14:1	59
14:2	59
14:3–5	59
14:9	59
14:11	59
14:12–15	59
14:16–19	59

APOCRYPHA

2 Maccabees

5—6	73

PSEUDEPIGRAPHA

1 Enoch

	13, 86–87, 115, 136, 139, 140, 142, 151
1–36	136, 138
1:9	142
10:4–6	86, 110
10:11–14	86, 151
14	140
14:1–7	86–87
17:9–16	86–87
17–19	146
22:2	86–87
54	86–87, 151

NEW TESTAMENT

Matthew

	116, 121
3	38
3:1–12	108
5:22	108
5:25–26	109
5:29	109
5:30	109
6:37–38	109
7:13–14	109
7:19	109
8:11	109
8:11–12	109
9:11–12	109
10:28	109
11:20–24	109
12:22–32	121
13:24–30	84–85
13:37–43	85

13:40	109	3:22–29	121
16:27	109	5:1–8	103
18:8	109	8:38	103
18:9	109	9:19	103
22:1–14	110	9:42	103
22:23–33	86, 125	9:43–48	7, 40
22:41–45	27	9:43	103, 109
23	110	9:45	103, 109
23:1–39	110	9:47	109
23:15	109	9:47–48	103
23:33–39	110–111	9:48	7
23:33	109	11:15–17	103
24	100	12:7–9	103
24:1–35	111	12:18–27	86, 125
24:1–2	111	12:35–37	27
24:3	111	12:36	104
24:4–8	111	12:38–40	104
24:14	120	13	100, 104–108
24:9–14	111	13:1–31	111
24:36–51	111	13:1–4	104
24:15–21	112	13:2	104, 108
24:15	76–77	13:5–37	105–108
24:22–28	112	13:5–8	107
24:29–31	112	13:9–11	107
24:32–35	112	13:10	120
24:36–39	112	13:14	76–77
24:40–41	112	13:19	104, 108
25:41	109	13:12–23	107
24:42–44	112	13:24–27	107
24:45–51	112	13:24–25	104
25:1–13	113	13:24	108
25:14–30	113	13:32–36	111
25:31–46	113–114, 162	14:21	104
25:41–46	162		
28:9–10	125	**Luke**	
			102, 109, 115–117
Mark		3:1–19	108
	7, 102, 104, 115, 121	3:1–18	38, 90–91
1:1–8	38	3:1–14	90–91
1:15	83–84	3:1–6	90
1:23–24	102	3:7–9	90
1:25	103	3:10–14	90
3:22–30	103	3:15–18	90–91

Luke - continued

4—14	91
4:33–35	91
6:37–38	91, 109
6:49	91
8:26–37	91
9:26	92
9:41	92
10:8–15	92, 96, 109
10:8–12	92
10:18	35
10:13–15	92
10:17–18	92
11:20	93
11:45–54	93
12:5	93
12:9	93
12:10	93, 121
12:13–21	93
12:24–46	93, 111
12:47–48	93, 122
12:58–59	93–94, 109
13:5	94
13:6–9	94
13:22–30	94, 109–110
14:16–24	94, 110
16—20	95–98
16:13–15	95
16:19–31	95–96
17:1–2	96
17:20–37	96
17:26–27	111
19:11–27	98
19:41–44	98
20:9–16	98
20:27–40	86, 125
20:41–44	27
20:42–43	98
20:45–47	98
21:5–38	98–102, 104
21:5–7	100
21:5	100
21:6	100
21:7	100
21:8–11	100
21:8	100
21:12–19	100–101
21:20–24	101, 108
21:25–28	101
21:29–33	101
21:34–36	101
21:37–38	101, 104
24:36–43	125
24:46–47	30
24:50–52	125

John

1:1–14	32
3:16	115
5:22–23	115
5:28–29	115
14:1–3	115
14:12	166
14:26	47
20:24–29	125
21:24–25	126

Acts

	117
1:3	140
1:1–11	117–118
1:9–11	125
3	118–120
3:1–26	117
3:1–10	118
3:11–26	118–120
3:23	120
7:1—8:1	93
7:51–60	117, 120–121
9:1–22	121
11:28	102, 107
16:26	102, 107
17:29–31	117, 121–122
21:27—28:31	101

Romans

	123
1:18—5:21	123
8:16	47
8:18–32	166

1 Corinthians

	123
3:10–15	123–124, 126, 157
15:50–58	124–125

2 Corinthians

12:1–10	126

Ephesians

6:12	80, 93, 140

Philippians

	123
2:5–11	130
2:6–8	130
2:9–11	130–131

Colossians

1:15–20	32

1 Thessalonians

	123
4:13–18	125–127, 157
5:1–11	125–127
5:3	128
5:1–3	127
5:4–11	127
4:13—5:11	129

2 Thessalonians

	123
1:6–10	127
1:9	127–128
2	141, 144, 157
2:1–12	5, 127–129, 144
2:1–2	129
2:3–4	129
2:3	129
2:4	129
2:5–12	129
2:8	128

1 Timothy

2:1–4	155

Hebrews

	47, 123
1	32
6:4–8	131
10:26–31	131
13:2	139

1 Peter

	133–134, 136, 153
1:10–12	8
3:18—4:6	132–140
3:18	133
3:19–20	132–140, 153
3:19	134
4:6	132–140
4:7	83

2 Peter

2	140–142
2:4	140
2:5	13
2:17	140
2:20–22	141
3:1–13	141
3:3–13	84
3:8–9	84, 141
3:11–12	120
3:11	141

1 John

	144
2:18	141
2:22	141
4:1–3	101
4:3	141

2 John

1:7	141

Jude

	132, 142
1:6	142
1:12	80
1:14–15	142

Revelation

	1, 5, 7, 48, 51–52, 60, 65, 67, 156, 164
1:5	157, 159–160
1:14	70
1:18	156
2:26	164
6—20	159
6:15	157
7:9–17	147
10:11	157, 164
11—21	144–152
11	166
11:1–6	144
11:7	144
11:8–10	145
11:11–19	145
11:18	165
12:1–6	145
12:5	164
12:7–17	146
12:7–9	93
12:9	12
13	146–147
13:1–4	146, 153
13:5–10	146
13:11–18	146
14—18	6–7, 144
14	147–148
14:6–19:3	156
14:6–13	147
14:6–11	156
14:6–8	156
14:7	147
14:8	147–148, 165
14:9–11	147, 156
15	148
15:2–4	158
15:4	165
15:5	165
16—20	159
16	148, 151
16:2	148
16:3	148
16:4–7	148
16:8–9	148
16:10–11	148
16:12–16	148, 158
16:16	51
16:17–21	51, 149
16:19	165
17	143, 149
17:1–2	149
17:2	158
17:3–6	149
17:3	143
17:6–8	149
17:8	143, 158
17:8–11	5
17:9–14	143–144
17:9–11	6, 70, 149
17:9–10	7
17:9	6
17:10	6
17:11	6
17:12–14	149–150
17:12	158
17:15–18	150
17:15	165

17:18	158
18	150
18:1–3	150
18:3	165
18:4–8	150
18:9–20	150
18:9	158
18:21–24	150
18:23	165
19	1, 151–152
19:11—20:15	51
19:11–21	51, 156
19:15	165
19:17–18	51, 158
19:20	156–157
19:20–21	158
20	159
20:1–10	151–152
20:1–7	151
20:3	165
20:4	156–157
20:8–10	151
20:8–9	165
20:7–10	52, 156
20:9	52
20:10–15	40
20:10	153, 157
20:11–15	156, 158
20:13–14	156
20:14–15	157
21—22	40
21:24–27	158
21:24–26	165
21:24	159
22	10
22:2	165
22:14-15	159–160

BABYLONIAN TALMUD

Book 2: Tract Rosh Hashana

1	88–90

JOSEPHUS

Wars of the Jews

Book 6

4	77
5	102

EARLY CHRISTIAN WRITINGS

Ecumenical Councils

Fifth Ecumenical Council
　　　　　　　　135–136, 154–155
Fourth Ecumenical Council
　　　　　　　　139
Nicene-Constantinople Creed
　　　　　　　　155, 163

Augustine

City of God

15:23	137
21:17	135, 160–161
21:23	154-155, 162
21:26	161
"Letter 164"	134–135, 154

Clement of Alexandria

Stromata

6:6	133

Evodius

"Letter 163"	134, 136

Gregory of Nyssa

Great Catechism

26	154, 161

"On the Soul and the Resurrection" 154
"On the Three Day Period" 134

Irenaeus

Against Heresies

4:27:2	133, 135
4:36:4	137

Origen

De Principiis

2:5	134
3:6:5	162

www.ingramcontent.com/pod-product-compliance
Lightning Source LLC
Chambersburg PA
CBHW050802160426
43192CB00010B/1609